The Little Book
of
Deep Learning

François

Contents

Contents   5

List of figures   7

Foreword   8

I   Foundations   10

1   Machine Learning   11
   1.1   Learning from data   12
   1.2   Basis function regression   14
   1.3   Under and overfitting   16
   1.4   Categories of models   18

2   Efficient computation   20
   2.1   GPUs, TPUs, and batches   21
   2.2   Tensors   23

3   Training   25
   3.1   Losses   26
   3.2   Autoregressive models   30
   3.3   Gradient descent   34

3.4 Backpropagation 39

3.5 The value of depth 44

3.6 Training protocols 47

3.7 The benefits of scale 50

II Deep models   55

4 Model components   56

4.1 The notion of layer 57

4.2 Linear layers 59

4.3 Activation functions 69

4.4 Pooling 72

4.5 Dropout 75

4.6 Normalizing layers 78

4.7 Skip connections 82

4.8 Attention layers 85

4.9 Token embedding 92

4.10 Positional encoding 93

5 Architectures   95

5.1 Multi-Layer Perceptrons 96

5.2 Convolutional networks 98

5.3 Attention models 105

III Applications   112

6 Prediction   113

6.1 Image denoising 114

6.2 Image classification 116

6.3 Object detection 117

6.4 Semantic segmentation 122

6.5 Speech recognition 125

6.6 Text-image representations . . . 127

7 Synthesis 130

7.1 Text generation 131

7.2 Image generation 133

The missing bits 137

Afterword 143

Bibliography 144

Index 153

List of Figures

1.1 Kernel regression 14
1.2 Overfitting of kernel regression . . 16

3.1 Causal autoregressive model 32
3.2 Gradient descent 35
3.3 Backpropagation 39
3.4 Feature warping 45
3.5 Train and validation losses 48
3.6 Scaling laws 51
3.7 Model training costs 53

4.1 1D convolution 61
4.2 2D convolution 62
4.3 Stride, padding, and dilation 63
4.4 Receptive field 66
4.5 Activation functions 70
4.6 Max pooling 73
4.7 Dropout 76
4.8 Batch normalization 79
4.9 Skip connections 83
4.10 Attention operator interpretation . 86

4.11 Complete attention operator 88

4.12 Multi-Head Attention layer 90

5.1 Multi-Layer Perceptron 96

5.2 LeNet-like convolutional model . . 99

5.3 Residual block 100

5.4 Downscaling residual block 101

5.5 ResNet-50 102

5.6 Self and cross-attention blocks . . . 106

5.7 Transformer 107

5.8 GPT model 109

5.9 ViT model 110

6.1 Convolutional object detector . . . 118

6.2 Object detection with SSD 119

6.3 Semantic segmentation with PSP . . 123

6.4 CLIP zero-shot prediction 129

7.1 Denoising diffusion 134

Foreword

The current period of progress in artificial intelligence was triggered when Krizhevsky et al. [2012] showed that an artificial neural network with a simple structure, which had been known for more than twenty years [LeCun et al., 1989], could beat complex state-of-the-art image recognition methods by a huge margin, simply by being a hundred times larger, and trained on a data set similarly scaled up.

This breakthrough was made possible thanks to Graphical Processing Units (GPUs), mass-market highly parallel computing devices developed for real-time image synthesis and repurposed for artificial neural networks.

Since then, under the umbrella term of "deep learning," innovations in the structures of these networks, the strategies to train them, and dedicated hardware have allowed for an exponential increase in both their size and the quantity of training data they take advantage of [Sevilla et al., 2022]. This has resulted in a wave of successful applications across technical domains, from computer vision and robotics, to speech, and natural language processing.

Although the bulk of deep learning is not particularly difficult to understand, it combines diverse components, which makes it complicated to learn. It involves multiple branches of mathematics such as calculus, probabilities, optimization, linear algebra, and signal processing, and it is also deeply anchored in computer science, programming, algorithmic, and high-performance computing.

Instead of trying to be exhaustive, this little book is limited to the background and tools necessary to understand a few important models.

If you did not get this book from its official URL

https://fleuret.org/public/lbdl.pdf

please do so, so that I can estimate the number of readers.

François Fleuret,
May 21, 2023

PART I

FOUNDATIONS

Chapter 1
Machine Learning

Deep learning belongs historically to the larger field of statistical machine learning, as it fundamentally concerns methods able to learn representations from data. The techniques involved come originally from artificial neural networks, and the "deep" qualifier highlights that models are long compositions of mappings, now known to achieve greater performance.

The modularity of deep models, their versatility, and scaling qualities, have resulted in a plethora of specific mathematical methods and software development tools that have established deep learning as a separate and vast technical field.

1.1 Learning from data

The simplest use case for a model trained from data is when a signal x is accessible, for instance, the picture of a license plate, from which one wants to predict a quantity y, such as the string of characters written on the plate.

In many real-world situations where x is a high-dimension signal captured in an uncontrolled environment, it is too complicated to come up with an analytical recipe that relates x and y.

What one can do is to collect a large training set $\mathscr{D}$ of pairs (x_n, y_n), and devise a parametric model f, a piece of computer code that incorporates trainable parameters w that modulate its behavior, and such that, with the proper values w^*, it is a good predictor. "Good" here means that if an x is given to this piece of code, the value $\hat{y} = f(x; w^*)$ it computes is a good estimate of the y that would have been associated to x in the training set had it been there.

This notion of goodness is usually formalized with a loss $\mathscr{L}(w)$ which is small when $f(\cdot; w)$ is good on $\mathscr{D}$. Then, training the model consists of computing a value w^* that minimizes $\mathscr{L}(w^*)$.

Most of the content of this book is about the definition of f which, in realistic scenarios, is a complex combination of pre-defined sub-modules.

The trainable parameters that compose w are often referred to as <u>weights</u>, by analogy with the synaptic weights of biological neural networks. In addition to these parameters, models usually depend on <u>meta-parameters</u> which are set according to domain prior knowledge, best practices, or resource constraints. They may also be optimized in some way, but with techniques different from those used to optimize w.

1.2 Basis function regression

We can illustrate the training of a model in a simple case where x_n and y_n are two real numbers, the loss is the mean squared error:

$$\mathcal{L}(w) = \frac{1}{N}\sum_{n=1}^{N}(y_n - f(x_n;w))^2, \qquad (1.1)$$

and $f(\cdot;w)$ is a linear combination of a predefined basis of functions $f_1, \ldots, f_K$, with $w = (w_1, \ldots, w_K)$:

$$f(x;w) = \sum_{k=1}^{K} w_k f_k(x).$$

Since $f(x_n;w)$ is linear with respect to the w_ks and $\mathcal{L}(w)$ is quadratic with respect to $f(x_n;w)$,

Figure 1.1: *Given a basis of functions (blue curves) and a training set (black dots), we can compute an optimal linear combination of the former (red curve) to approximate the latter for the mean squared error.*

the loss $\mathscr{L}(w)$ is quadratic with respect to the w_ks, and finding w^* that minimizes it boils down to solving a linear system. See Figure 1.1 for an example with Gaussian kernels as f_k.

1.3 Under and overfitting

A key element is the interplay between the capacity of the model, that is its flexibility and ability to fit diverse data, and the amount and quality of the training data. When the capacity is insufficient, the model cannot fit the data and the error during training is high. This is referred to as underfitting.

On the contrary, when the amount of data is insufficient, as illustrated with an example in Figure 1.2, the performance during training can be excellent, but unrelated to the actual fit to the data structure, as in that case the model will often learn random noise present in the signal.

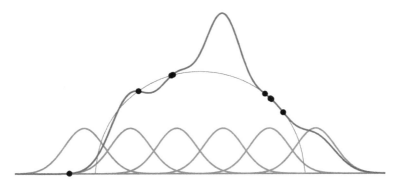

Figure 1.2: *If the amount of training data is small compared to the capacity of the model, the performance during training reflects poorly the actual fit to the underlying data structure, and consequently the usefulness for prediction.*

This is overfitting.

So, a large part of the art of applied machine learning is to design models that are not too flexible yet still able to fit the data. This is done by crafting the right inductive bias in a model, which means that its structure corresponds to the underlying structure of the data at hand.

Even though this classical perspective is relevant for reasonably-sized deep models, things get confusing with large ones that have a very large number of trainable parameters and extreme capacity yet still perform well for prediction. We will come back to this in § 3.6.

1.4 Categories of models

We can organize the use of machine learning models into three broad categories:

- Regression consists of predicting a continuous-valued vector $y \in \mathbb{R}^K$, for instance, a geometrical position of an object, given an input signal X. This is a multi-dimensional generalization of the setup we saw in § 1.2. The training set is composed of pairs of an input signal and a ground-truth value.

- Classification aims at predicting a value from a finite set $\{1, \ldots, C\}$, for instance, the label Y of an image X. As for regression, the training set is composed of pairs of input signal, and ground-truth quantity, here a label from that set. The standard way of tackling this is to predict one score per potential class, such that the correct class has the maximum score.

- Density modeling has as its objective to model the probability density function of the data μ_X itself, for instance, images. In that case, the training set is composed of values x_n without associated quantities to predict, and the trained model should allow either the evaluation of the probability density function, or sampling from the distribution, or both.

Both regression and classification are generally referred to as supervised learning since the value to be predicted, which is required as a target during training, has to be provided, for instance, by human experts. On the contrary, density modeling is usually seen as unsupervised learning since it is sufficient to take existing data, without the need for producing an associated ground-truth.

These three categories are not disjoint; for instance, classification can be cast as class-score regression, or discrete sequence density modeling as iterated classification. Furthermore, they do not cover all cases. One may want to predict compounded quantities, or multiple classes, or model a density conditional on a signal.

Chapter *2*

Efficient computation

From an implementation standpoint, deep learning is about executing heavy computations with large amounts of data. The Graphical Processing Units (GPUs) have been instrumental in the success of the field by allowing such computations to be run on affordable hardware.

The importance of their use, and the resulting technical constraints on the computations that can be done efficiently, force the research in the field to constantly balance mathematical soundness and implementability of novel methods.

2.1 GPUs, TPUs, and batches

Graphical Processing Units were originally designed for real-time image synthesis, which requires highly parallel architectures that happen to be fitting for deep models. As their usage for AI has increased, GPUs have been equipped with dedicated sub-components referred to as tensor cores, and deep-learning specialized chips such as Google's Tensor Processing Units (TPUs) have been developed.

A GPU possesses several thousands of parallel units, and its own fast memory. The limiting factor is usually not the number of computing units but the read-write operations to memory. The slowest link is between the CPU memory and the GPU memory, and consequently one should avoid copying data across devices. Moreover, the structure of the GPU itself involves multiple levels of cache memory, which are smaller but faster, and computation should be organized to avoid copies between these different caches.

This is achieved, in particular, by organizing the computation in batches of samples that can fit entirely in the GPU memory and are processed in parallel. When an operator combines a sample and model parameters, both have to be moved to the cache memory near the actual computing units. Proceeding by batches allows for copying the model parameters only once, instead of doing it for every sample. In practice, a GPU processes a batch that fits in memory almost as quickly as a single sample.

A standard GPU has a theoretical peak performance of 10^{13}-10^{14} floating point operations (FLOPs) per second, and its memory typically ranges from 8 to 80 gigabytes. The standard FP32 encoding of float numbers is on 32 bits, but empirical results show that using encoding on 16 bits, or even less for some operands, does not degrade performance.

We come back in § 3.7 to the large size of deep architectures.

2.2 Tensors

GPUs and deep learning frameworks such as PyTorch or JAX manipulate the quantities to be processed by organizing them as tensors, which are series of scalars arranged along several discrete axes. They are elements of $\mathbb{R}^{N_1 \times \cdots \times N_D}$ that generalize the notion of vector and matrix.

Tensors are used to represent both the signals to process, the trainable parameters of the models, and the intermediate quantities they compute. The latters are called activations, in reference to neuronal activations.

For instance, a time series is naturally encoded as a $T \times D$ tensor, or, for historical reasons, as a $D \times T$ tensor, where T is its duration and D is the dimension of the feature representation at every time step, often referred to as the number of channels. Similarly a 2D-structured signal can be represented as a $D \times H \times W$ tensor, where H and W are its width and height. An RGB image would correspond to $D = 3$, but the number of channels can grow up to several thousands in large models.

Adding more dimensions allows for the representation of series of objects. Fifty RGB images of resolution 32×24 can, for instance, be encoded as a $50 \times 3 \times 24 \times 32$ tensor.

Deep learning libraries all provide a large number of operations that encompass standard linear algebra, complex reshaping and extraction, and deep-learning specific operations, some of which we will see in Chapter 4. The implementation of tensors separates the shape representation from the storage layout of the coefficients in memory, which allows many reshaping, transposing, and extraction operations to be done without coefficient copying, hence extremely rapidly.

In practice, virtually any computation can be decomposed into elementary tensor operations, which avoids non-parallel loops at the language level and poor memory management.

Besides being convenient tools, tensors are instrumental to achieve computational efficiency. All the people involved in the development of an operational deep model, from the designers of the drivers, libraries, and models to those of the computers and chips, know that the data will be manipulated as tensors. The resulting constraints on locality and block decomposability enable all the actors in this chain to come up with optimal designs.

Chapter 3

Training

As introduced in § 1.1, training a model consists of minimizing a loss $\mathcal{L}(w)$ which reflects the performance of the predictor $f(\cdot\,;w)$ on a training set $\mathcal{D}$. Since the models are usually extremely complex, and their performance is directly related to how well the loss is minimized, this minimization is a key challenge, which involves both computational and mathematical difficulties.

3.1 Losses

The example of the <u>mean squared error</u> of Equation 1.1 is a standard loss for predicting a continuous value.

For density modeling, the standard loss is the likelihood of the data. If $f(x;w)$ is to be interpreted as a normalized log-probability or log-density, the loss is the opposite of the sum of its value over training samples.

Cross-entropy

For <u>classification</u>, the usual strategy is that the output of the model is a vector with one component $f(x;w)_y$ per class y, interpreted as the logarithm of a non-normalized probability, or <u>logit</u>.

With X the input signal and Y the class to predict, we can then compute from f an estimate of the <u>posterior probabilities</u>:

$$\hat{P}(Y = y \mid X = x) = \frac{\exp f(x;w)_y}{\sum_z \exp f(x;w)_z}.$$

This expression is generally referred to as the <u>softmax</u>, or more adequately, the <u>softargmax</u>, of the logits.

To be consistent with this interpretation the model should be trained to maximize the probability of the true classes, hence to minimize the cross-entropy, expressed as:

$$\mathscr{L}_{\text{ce}}(w) = -\frac{1}{N} \sum_{n=1}^{N} \log \hat{P}(Y = y_n \mid X = x_n)$$

$$= \frac{1}{N} \sum_{n=1}^{N} \underbrace{-\log \frac{\exp f(x_n; w)_{y_n}}{\sum_z \exp f(x_n; w)_z}}_{L_{\text{ce}}(f(x_n; w), y_n)}.$$

Contrastive loss

In certain setups, even though the value to be predicted is continuous, the supervision takes the form of ranking constraints. The typical domain where this is the case is metric learning, where the objective is to learn a measure of distance between samples such that a sample x_a from a certain semantic class is closer to any sample x_b of the same class than to any sample x_c from another class. For instance, x_a and x_b can be two pictures of a certain person, and x_c a picture of someone else.

The standard approach for such cases is to minimize a contrastive loss, in that case, for instance, the sum over triplets (x_a, x_b, x_c), such that $y_a = y_b \neq y_c$, of

$$\max(0, 1 - f(x_a, x_c; w) + f(x_a, x_b; w)).$$

This quantity will be strictly positive unless $f(x_a, x_c; w) \geq 1 + f(x_a, x_b; w)$.

Engineering the loss

Usually, the loss minimized during training is not the actual quantity one wants to optimize ultimately, but a proxy for which finding the best model parameters is easier. For instance, cross-entropy is the standard loss for classification, even though the actual performance measure is a classification error rate, because the latter has no informative gradient, a key requirement as we will see in § 3.3.

It is also possible to add terms to the loss that depend on the trainable parameters of the model themselves to favor certain configurations.

The weight decay regularization, for instance, consists of adding to the loss a term proportional to the sum of the squared parameters. It can be interpreted as having a Gaussian Bayesian prior on the parameters, which favors smaller values and reduces the influence of the data. This degrades performance on the training set, but reduces the gap between the performance in training and that on new, unseen data.

3.2 Autoregressive models

Many spectacular applications in computer vision and natural language processing have been tackled with autoregressive models of discrete sequences.

The chain rule

Such models put to use the chain rule from probability theory:

$$
\begin{aligned}
P(X_1 = x_1, X_2 = x_2, \ldots, X_T = x_T) = \\
P(X_1 = x_1) \\
\times P(X_2 = x_2 \mid X_1 = x_1) \\
\ldots \\
\times P(X_T = x_T \mid X_1 = x_1, \ldots, X_{T-1} = x_{T-1}).
\end{aligned}
$$

Although it is valid for any type of random quantity, this decomposition finds its most efficient use when the signal of interest can be encoded into a sequence of discrete tokens from a finite vocabulary $\{1, \ldots K\}$.

With the convention that the additional token $\emptyset$ stands for an "unknown" quantity, we can represent the event $\{X_1 = x_1, \ldots, X_t = x_t\}$ as the vector $(x_1, \ldots, x_t, \emptyset, \ldots, \emptyset)$.

Then, given a model

$$f(x_1,\ldots,x_{t-1},\emptyset,\ldots,\emptyset;w) = \\ \log \hat{P}(X_t \mid X_1 = x_1,\ldots,X_{t-1} = x_{t-1}),$$

the chain rule states that one can sample a full sequence of length T by sampling the x_ts one after another, each according to the predicted posterior distribution, given the $x_1,\ldots,x_{t-1}$ already sampled. This is an <u>autoregressive</u> generative model.

Causal models

Training such a model could be achieved naively by minimizing the sum across training sequences x and time steps t of

$$L_{\text{ce}}\big(f(x_1,\ldots,x_{t-1},\emptyset,\ldots,\emptyset;w),x_t\big),$$

however such an approach is inefficient, as most computations done for $t < t'$ have to be repeated for t'.

The standard strategy to address this issue is to design a model f that predicts the distributions of all the x_t of the sequence at once, but which has a structure such that the computed logits for e.g. x_t depend only on the input values $x_1,\ldots,x_{t-1}$. Such a model is called <u>causal</u>,

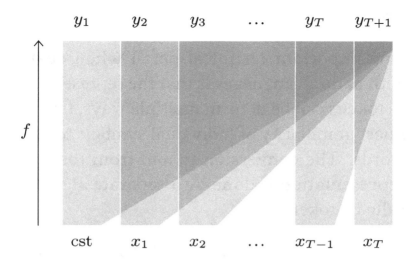

$$y_1 \quad y_2 \quad y_3 \quad \cdots \quad y_T \quad y_{T+1}$$

f

$$\text{cst} \quad x_1 \quad x_2 \quad \cdots \quad x_{T-1} \quad x_T$$

Figure 3.1: *An autoregressive model f, is causal if a time step x_t of the input sequence can only modulate a predicted $y_s = \hat{P}(X_s \mid X_{t<s})$ for $s > t$.*

since it corresponds in the case of temporal series to not letting the future influence the past, as illustrated in Figure 3.1.

The consequence is that the output at every position is the one that would be obtained if the input was only available up to before that position. Hence, training can be done by computing the output for a full training sequence, and maximizing the predicted probabilities of all the tokens of that same sequence, which boils down to minimizing the sum of the per-token cross-entropy.

Tokenizer

One important technical detail when dealing with natural languages is that the representation as tokens can be done in multiple ways, from the finest granularity of individual symbols to entire words. The conversion to and from the token representation is done by a separate algorithm called a tokenizer.

A standard method is the Byte Pair Encoding (BPE) [Sennrich et al., 2015] that constructs tokens by hierarchically merging groups of characters, trying to get tokens that represent fragments of words of various lengths but of similar frequencies, allocating tokens to long frequent fragments, as well as to rare individual symbols.

3.3   Gradient descent

Except in specific cases like the linear regression we saw in § 1.2, the optimal parameters w^* do not have a closed-form expression. In the general case, the tool of choice to minimize a function is gradient descent. It starts by initializing the parameters with a random w_0, and then improves this estimate by iterating gradient steps, each consisting of computing the gradient of the loss with respect to the parameters, and subtracting a fraction of it:

$$w_{n+1} = w_n - \eta \nabla \mathscr{L}_{|w}(w_n). \qquad (3.1)$$

This procedure corresponds to moving the current estimate a bit in the direction that locally decrease $\mathscr{L}(w)$ maximally, as illustrated in Figure 3.2.

Learning rate

The meta-parameter η is referred to as the learning rate. It is a positive value that modulates how quickly the minimization is done, and has to be chosen carefully.

If it is too small, the optimization will be slow at best, and may be trapped in a local minimum early. If it is too large, the optimization may

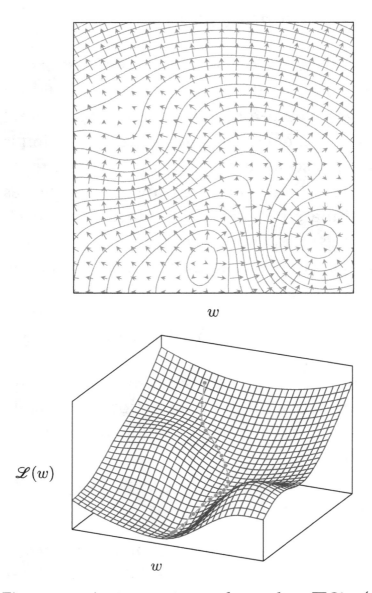

w

$\mathcal{L}(w)$

w

Figure 3.2: *At every point w, the gradient $\nabla\mathcal{L}_{|w}(w)$ is in the direction that maximizes the increase of $\mathcal{L}$, orthogonal to the level curves (top). The gradient descent minimizes $\mathcal{L}(w)$ iteratively by subtracting a fraction of the gradient at every step, resulting in a trajectory that follows the steepest descent (bottom).*

bounce around a good minimum and never descend into it. As we will see in § 3.6, it can depend on the iteration number n.

Stochastic Gradient Descent

All the losses used in practice can be expressed as an average of a loss per sample, or per small group of samples:

$$\mathscr{L}(w) = \frac{1}{N} \sum_{n=1}^{N} \ell_n(w),$$

where $\ell_n(w) = L(f(x_n; w), y_n)$ for some L, and the gradient is then:

$$\nabla\mathscr{L}_{|w}(w) = \frac{1}{N} \sum_{n=1}^{N} \nabla\ell_{n|w}(w). \qquad (3.2)$$

The resulting gradient descent would compute exactly the sum in Equation 3.2, which is usually computationally heavy, and then update the parameters according to Equation 3.1. However, under reasonable assumptions of exchangeability, for instance, if the samples have been properly shuffled, any partial sum of Equation 3.2 is an unbiased estimator of the full sum, albeit noisy. So, updating the parameters from partial sums corresponds to doing more gradient steps for the same computational budget, with noisier estimates of the gradient. Due to the redundancy in the data, this happens to be a far more efficient strategy.

We saw in § 2.1 that processing a batch of samples small enough to fit in the computing device's memory is generally as fast as processing a single one. Hence, the standard approach is to split the full set $\mathscr{D}$ into batches, and to update the parameters from the estimate of the gradient computed from each. This is referred to as mini-batch stochastic gradient descent, or stochastic gradient descent (SGD) for short.

It is important to note that this process is extremely gradual, and that the number of mini-batches and gradient steps are typically of the order of several millions.

As with many algorithms, intuition breaks down in high dimensions, and although it may seem that this procedure would be easily trapped in a local minimum, in reality, due to the number of parameters, the design of the models, and the stochasticity of the data, its efficiency is far greater than one might expect.

Plenty of variations of this standard strategy have been proposed. The most popular one is

<u>Adam</u> [Kingma and Ba, 2014], which keeps running estimates of the mean and variance of each component of the gradient, and normalizes them automatically, avoiding scaling issues and different training speeds in different parts of a model.

3.4 Backpropagation

Using gradient descent requires a technical means to compute $\nabla \ell_{|w}(w)$ where $\ell = L(f(x; w); y)$. Given that f and L are both compositions of standard tensor operations, as for any mathematical expression, the chain rule from differential calculus allows us to get an expression of it.

For the sake of making notation lighter–which, unfortunately, will be needed in what follows– we do not specify at which point gradients are computed, since the context makes it clear.

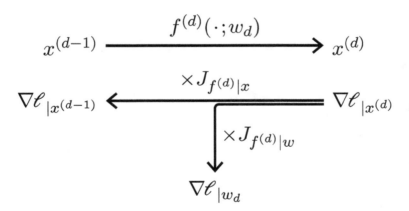

Figure 3.3: *Given a model $f = f^{(D)} \circ \cdots \circ f^{(1)}$, the forward pass (top) consists of computing the outputs $x^{(d)}$ of the mappings $f^{(d)}$ in order. The backward pass (bottom) computes the gradients of the loss with respect to the activation $x^{(d)}$ and the parameters w_d backward by multiplying them by the Jacobians.*

Forward and backward passes

Consider the simple case of a composition of mappings:

$$f = f^{(1)} \circ f^{(2)} \circ \cdots \circ f^{(D)}.$$

The output of $f(x; w)$ can be computed by starting with $x^{(0)} = x$ and applying iteratively:

$$x^{(d)} = f^{(d)}\left(x^{(d-1)}; w_d\right),$$

with $x^{(D)}$ as the final value.

The individual scalar values of these intermediate results $x^{(d)}$ are traditionally called activations in reference to neuron activations, the value D is the depth of the model, the individual mappings $f^{(d)}$ are referred to as layers, as we will see is § 4.1, and their sequential evaluation is the forward pass (see Figure 3.3, top).

Conversely, the gradient $\nabla \ell_{|x^{(d-1)}}$ of the loss with respect to the output $x^{(d-1)}$ of $f^{(d-1)}$ is the product of the gradient $\nabla \ell_{|x^{(d)}}$ with respect to the output of $f^{(d)}$ multiplied by the Jacobian $J_{f^{(d-1)}|x}$ of $f^{(d-1)}$ with respect to its variable x. Thus, the gradients with respect to the outputs of all the $f^{(d)}$s can be computed recursively backward, starting with $\nabla \ell_{|x^{(D)}} = \nabla L_{|x}$.

And the gradient that we are interested in for training, that is $\nabla \ell_{|w_d}$, is the gradient with respect to the output of $f^{(d)}$ multiplied by the Jacobian $J_{f^{(d)}|w}$ of $f^{(d)}$ with respect to the parameters.

This iterative computation of the gradients with respect to the intermediate activations, combined with that of the gradients with respect to the layers' parameters, is the backward pass (see Figure 3.3, bottom). The combination of this computation with the procedure of gradient descent is called backpropagation.

In practice, the implementation details of the forward and backward passes are hidden from programmers. Deep learning frameworks are able to automatically construct the sequence of operations to compute gradients. A particularly convenient algorithm is Autograd [Baydin et al., 2015], which tracks tensor operations and builds, on the fly, the combination of operators for gradients. Thanks to this, a piece of imperative programming that manipulates tensors can automatically compute the gradient of any quantity with respect to any other.

Resource usage

Regarding the computational cost, as we will see, the bulk of the computation goes into linear operations that require one matrix product for the forward pass and two for the products by the Jacobians for the backward pass, making the latter roughly twice as costly as the former.

The memory requirement during inference is roughly equal to that of the most demanding individual layer. For training, however, the backward pass requires keeping the activations computed during the forward pass to compute the Jacobians, which results in a memory usage that grows proportionally to the model's depth. Techniques exist to trade the memory usage for computation by either relying on reversible layers [Gomez et al., 2017], or using checkpointing, which consists of storing activations for some layers only and recomputing the others on the fly with partial forward passes during the backward pass [Chen et al., 2016].

Vanishing gradient

A key historical issue when training a large network is that when the gradient propagates backwards through an operator, it may be rescaled by a multiplicative factor, and consequently decrease or increase exponentially when it traverses many layer. When it decreases exponentially, this is called the vanishing gradient, and it may make the training impossible, or, in its milder form, cause different parts of the model to be updated at different speeds, degrading their co-adaptation [Glorot and Bengio, 2010].

As we will see in Chapter 4, multiple techniques have been developed to prevent this from happening, reflecting a change in perspective that was crucial to the success of deep-learning: instead of trying to improve generic optimization methods, the effort shifted to engineering the models themselves to make them optimizable.

3.5 The value of depth

As the term "deep learning" indicates, useful models are generally compositions of long series of mappings. Training them with gradient descent results in a sophisticated co-adaptation of the mappings, even though this procedure is gradual and local.

We can illustrate this behavior with a simple model $\mathbb{R}^2 \to \mathbb{R}^2$ that combines eight layers, each multiplying its input by a 2×2 matrix and applying Tanh per component, with a final linear classifier. This is a simplified Multi-Layer Perceptron (see § 5.1).

If we train this model with SGD and cross-entropy on a toy binary classification task (Figure 3.4, top-left), the matrices co-adapt to deform the space until the classification is correct, which implies that the data have been made linearly separable before the final affine operation (Figure 3.4, bottom-right).

Such an example gives a glimpse of what a deep model can achieve; however, it is partially misleading due to the low dimension of both the signal to process and the internal representations. Everything is kept in 2D here for the sake of visualization, while real models take advantage

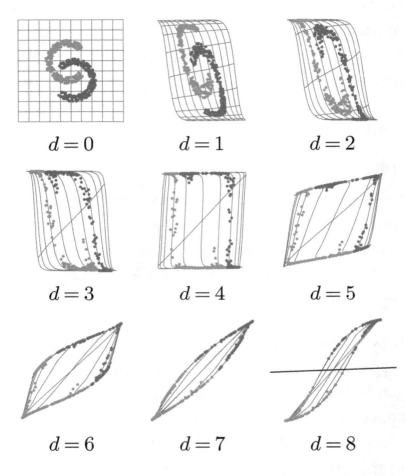

Figure 3.4: *Each plot shows the deformation of the space and the resulting positioning of the training points in $\mathbb{R}^2$ after d layers of processing, starting with the input to the model itself (top-left). The oblique line in the last plot (bottom-right) shows the final affine decision.*

of representations in high dimensions, which, in particular, facilitates the optimization by providing many degrees of freedom.

Empirical evidence accumulated over twenty years demonstrates that state-of-the-art performance across application domains necessitates models with tens of layers, such as residual networks (see § 5.2) and Transformers (see § 5.3).

Theoretical results show that for a fixed computational budget or number of parameters, increasing the depth leads to a greater complexity of the resulting mapping [Telgarsky, 2016].

3.6 Training protocols

Training a deep network requires defining a protocol to make the most of computation and data, and ensure that performance will be good on new data.

As we saw in § 1.3, the performance on the training samples may be misleading, so in the simplest setup one needs at least two sets of samples: one is a training set, used to optimize the model parameters, and the other is a test set, to estimate the performance of the trained model.

Additionally, there are usually meta-parameters to adapt, in particular, those related to the model architecture, the learning rate, and the regularization terms in the loss. In that case, one needs a validation set that is disjoint from both the training set and the test set to assess the best configuration.

The full training is usually decomposed into epochs, each of them corresponding to going through all the training examples once. The usual dynamic of the losses is that the train loss decreases as long as the optimization runs while the validation loss may reach a minimum after a certain number of epochs and then start to increase, reflecting an overfitting regime, as in-

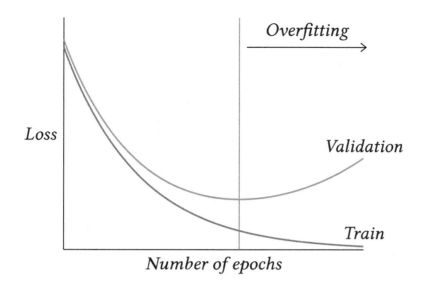

Figure 3.5: *As training progresses, a model's perfor-mance is usually monitored through losses. The train loss is the one driving the optimization process and goes down, while the validation loss is estimated on an other set of examples to assess the overfitting of the model. Overfitting appears when the model starts to take into account random structures specific to the training set at hands, resulting in the validation loss starting to increase.*

troduced in § 1.3 and illustrated on Figure 3.5.

Paradoxically, although they should suffer from severe overfitting due to their capacity, large models usually continue to improve as training progresses. This may be due to the inductive bias of the model becoming the main driver of optimization when performance is near perfect on the training set [Belkin et al., 2018].

An important design choice is the learning rate schedule during training. The general policy is that the learning rate should be initially large to avoid having the optimization being trapped in a bad local minimum early, and that it should get smaller so that the optimized parameter values do not bounce around, and reach a good minimum in a narrow valley of the loss landscape.

The training of extremely large models may take months on thousands of powerful GPUs and have a financial cost of several million dollars. At this scale, the training may involve many manual interventions informed, in particular, by the dynamics of the loss evolution.

3.7 The benefits of scale

There is an accumulation of empirical results showing that performance, for instance, estimated through the loss on test data, improves with the amount of data according to remarkable scaling laws, as long as the model size increases correspondingly [Kaplan et al., 2020] (see Figure 3.6).

Benefiting from these scaling laws in the multi-billion samples regime is possible in part thanks to the structural plasticity of models, which allows them to be scaled up arbitrarily, as we will see, by increasing the number of layers or feature dimensions. But it is also made possible by the distributed nature of the computation implemented by these models and by stochastic gradient descent, which requires only a tiny fraction of the data at a time and can operate with data sets whose size is orders of magnitude greater than that of the computing device's memory. This has resulted in an exponential growth of the models, as illustrated in Figure 3.7.

Typical vision models have 10–100 million trainable parameters and require 10^{18}–10^{19} FLOPs for training [He et al., 2015; Sevilla et al., 2022]. Language models have from 100 million to hun-

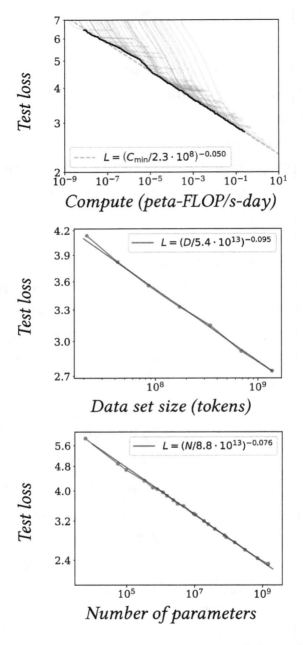

Figure 3.6: *Test loss of a language model vs. the amount of computation in petaflop/s-day, the data set size in tokens, that is fragments of words, and the model size in parameters [Kaplan et al., 2020].*

Dataset	Year	Nb. of images	Size
ImageNet	2012	1.2M	150Gb
Cityscape	2016	25K	60Gb
LAION-5B	2022	5.8B	240Tb

Dataset	Year	Nb. of books	Size
WMT-18-de-en	2018	14M	8Gb
The Pile	2020	1.6B	825Gb
OSCAR	2020	12B	6Tb

Table 3.1: *Some examples of publicly available datasets. The equivalent number of books is an indicative estimate for 250 pages of 2000 characters per book.*

dreds of billions of trainable parameters and require 10^{20}–10^{23} FLOPs for training [Devlin et al., 2018; Brown et al., 2020; Chowdhery et al., 2022; Sevilla et al., 2022]. The latter require machines with multiple high-end GPUs.

Training these large models is impossible using datasets with a detailed ground-truth costly to produce, which can only be of moderate size. Instead, it is done with datasets automatically produced by combining data available on the internet with minimal curation, if any. These sets may combine multiple modalities, such as text and images from web pages, or sound and images from videos, which can be used for large-scale supervised training.

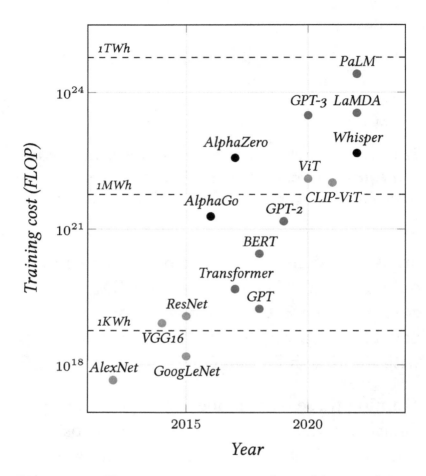

Figure 3.7: *Training costs in number of FLOP of some landmark models [Sevilla et al., 2023]. The colors indicate the domains of application: Computer Vision (blue), Natural Language Processing (red), or other (black). The dashed lines correspond to the energy consumption using A100s SXM in 16 bits precision.*

The most impressive current successes of artificial intelligence rely on the so-called <u>Large Language Models</u> (LLMs), which we will see in § 5.3 and § 7.1, trained on extremely large text datasets (see Table 3.1).

PART II

DEEP MODELS

Chapter 4
Model components

A deep model is nothing more than a complex tensorial computation that can be decomposed ultimately into standard mathematical operations from linear algebra and analysis. Over the years, the field has developed a large collection of high-level modules that have a clear semantic, and complex models combining these modules, which have proven to be effective in specific application domains.

Empirical evidence and theoretical results show that greater performance is achieved with deeper architectures, that is, long compositions of mappings. As we saw in section § 3.4, training such a model is challenging due to the vanishing gradient, and multiple important technical contributions have mitigated this problem.

4.1   The notion of layer

We call layers standard complex compounded tensor operations that have been designed and empirically identified as being generic and efficient. They often incorporate trainable parameters and correspond to a convenient level of granularity for designing and describing large deep models. The term is inherited from simple multi-layer neural networks, even though modern models may take the form of a complex graph of such modules, incorporating multiple parallel pathways.

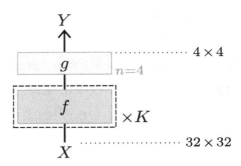

In the following pages, I try to stick to the convention for model depiction illustrated above:

• operators / layers are depicted as boxes,

• darker coloring indicates that they embed trainable parameters,

• non-default valued meta-parameters are

added in blue on their right,

- a dashed outer frame with a multiplicative factor indicates that a group of layers is replicated in series, each with its own set of trainable parameters if any, and

- in some cases, the dimension of their output is specified on the right when it differs from their input.

Additionally, layers that have a complex internal structure are depicted with a greater height.

4.2 Linear layers

The most important modules in terms of computation and number of parameters are the Linear
layers. They benefit from decades of research
and engineering in algorithmic and chip design
for matrix operations.

Note that the term "linear" in deep learning generally improperly refers to an affine operation,
that is the sum of a linear expression and a constant bias.

Fully connected layers

The most basic linear layer is the fully connected
layer, parameterized by a trainable weight matrix W of size $D' \times D$ and bias vector b of dimension D'. It implements an affine transformation
generalized to arbitrary tensor shapes, where
the supplementary dimensions are interpreted
as vector indexes. Formally, given an input X
of dimension $D_1 \times \cdots \times D_K \times D$, it computes an
output Y of dimension $D_1 \times \cdots \times D_K \times D'$ with

$$\forall d_1, \ldots, d_K,$$
$$Y[d_1, \ldots, d_K] = W X[d_1, \ldots, d_K] + b.$$

While at first sight such an affine operation

seems limited to geometric transformations such as rotations, symmetries, and translations, it can in facts do more than that. In particular, projections for dimension reduction or signal filtering, but also, from the perspective of the dot product being a measure of similarity, a matrix-vector product can be interpreted as computing matching scores between the queries, as encoded by the input vectors, and keys, as encoded by the matrix rows.

As we saw in § 3.3, the gradient descent starts with the parameters' random initialization. If this is done too naively, as seen in § 3.4, the network may suffer from exploding or vanishing activations and gradients [Glorot and Bengio, 2010]. Deep learning frameworks implement initialization methods that in particular scale the random parameters according to the dimension of the input to keep the variance of the activations constant and prevent pathological behaviors.

Convolutional layers

A linear layer can take as input an arbitrarily-shaped tensor by reshaping it into a vector, as long as it has the correct number of coefficients. However, such a layer is poorly adapted to deal-

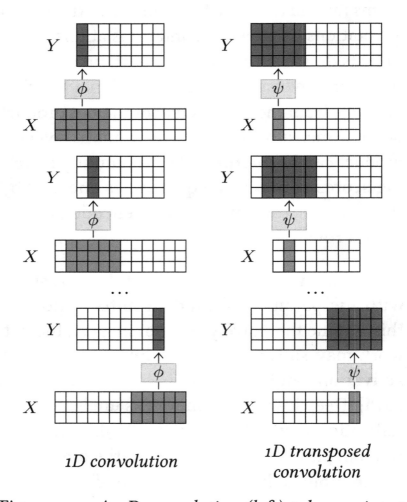

1D convolution

1D transposed convolution

Figure 4.1: *A 1D convolution (left) takes as input a $D \times T$ tensor X, applies the same affine mapping $\phi(\cdot\,;w)$ to every sub-tensor of shape $D \times K$, and stores the resulting $D' \times 1$ tensors into Y. A 1D transposed convolution (right) takes as input a $D \times T$ tensor, applies the same affine mapping $\psi(\cdot\,;w)$ to every sub-tensor of shape $D \times 1$, and sums the shifted resulting $D' \times K$ tensors. Both can process inputs of different size.*

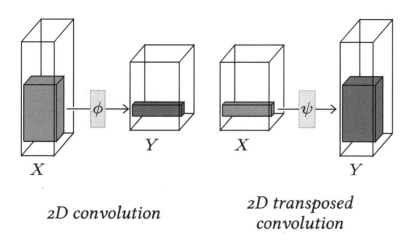

Figure 4.2: *A 2D convolution (left) takes as input a $D \times H \times W$ tensor X, applies the same affine mapping $\phi(\,\cdot\,; w)$ to every sub-tensor of shape $D \times K \times L$, and stores the resulting $D' \times 1 \times 1$ tensors into Y. A 2D transposed convolution (right) takes as input a $D \times H \times W$ tensor, applies the same affine mapping $\psi(\,\cdot\,; w)$ to every $D \times 1 \times 1$ sub-tensor, and sums the shifted resulting $D' \times K \times L$ tensors into Y.*

ing with large tensors, since the number of parameters and number of operations are proportional to the product of the input and output dimensions. For instance, to process an RGB image of size 256×256 as input and compute a result of the same size, it would require approximately 4×10^{10} parameters and multiplications.

Besides these practical issues, most of the high-dimension signals are strongly structured. For instance, images exhibit short-term correlations

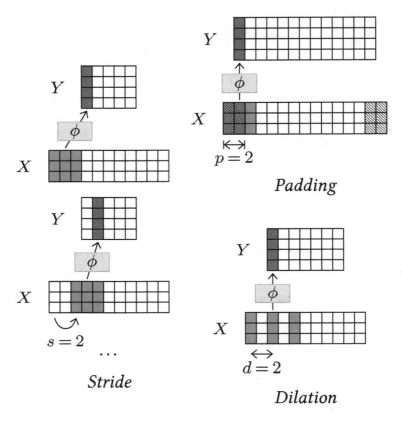

Figure 4.3: *Beside its kernel size and number of input / output channels, a convolution admits three meta-parameters: the stride s (left) modulates the step size when going though the input tensor, the padding p (top right) specifies how many zeros entries are added around the input tensor before processing it, and the dilation d (bottom right) parameterizes the index count between coefficients of the filter.*

and statistical stationarity to translation, scaling, and certain symmetries. This is not reflected in the <u>inductive bias</u> of a fully connected layer, which completely ignores the signal structure.

To leverage these regularities, the tool of choice is <u>convolutional layers</u>, which are also affine, but process time-series or 2D signals locally, with the same operator everywhere.

A <u>1D convolution</u> is mainly defined by three meta-parameters: its <u>kernel size</u> K, its number of input channels D, its number of output channels D', and by the trainable parameters w of an affine mapping $\phi(\cdot\,; w) : \mathbb{R}^{D \times K} \to \mathbb{R}^{D' \times 1}$.

It can process any tensor X of size $D \times T$ with $T \geq K$, and applies $\phi(\cdot\,; w)$ to every sub-tensor $D \times K$ of X, storing the results in a tensor Y of size $D' \times (T - K + 1)$, as pictured in Figure 4.1 (left).

A <u>2D convolution</u> is similar but has a $K \times L$ kernel and takes as input a $D \times H \times W$ tensor (see Figure 4.2, left).

Both operators have for trainable parameters those of ϕ that can be envisioned as D' <u>filters</u> of size $D \times K$ or $D \times K \times L$ respectively, and a <u>bias vector</u> of dimension D'.

They also admit three additional meta-parameters, illustrated on Figure 4.3:

• The padding specifies how many zero coefficients should be added around the input tensor before processing it, particularly to maintain the tensor size when the kernel size is greater than one. Its default value is 0.

• The stride specifies the step used when going through the input, allowing one to reduce the output size geometrically by using large steps. Its default value is 1.

• The dilation specifies the index count between the filter coefficients of the local affine operator. Its default value is 1, and greater values correspond to inserting zeros between the coefficients, which increases the filter / kernel size while keeping the number of trainable parameters unchanged.

Except for the number of channels, a convolution's output is usually strictly smaller than its input by roughly the size of the kernel, or even by a scaling factor if the stride is greater than one.

Given an activation computed by a convolutional layer, or the vector of values for all the channels

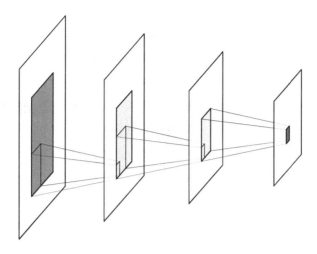

Figure 4.4: *Given an activation in a series of convolution layers, here in red, its <u>receptive field</u> is the area in the input signal, in blue, that modulates its value. Each intermediate convolutional layer increases the width and height of that area by roughly those of the kernel.*

at a certain location, the portion of the input signal that it depends on is called its <u>receptive field</u> (see Figure 4.4). One of the $H \times W$ sub-tensors corresponding to a single channel of a $D \times H \times W$ activation tensor is referred to as an <u>activation map</u>.

Convolutions are used to recombine information, generally to reduce the spatial size of the representation, trading it for a greater number of channels, which translates into a richer local representation. They can implement differential operators such as edge-detectors, or template matching mechanisms. A succession of such layers can also be envisioned as a compositional and hierarchical representation [Zeiler and Fergus, 2014], or as a diffusion process in which information can be transported by half the kernel size when passing through a layer.

A converse operation is the <u>transposed convolution</u> that also consists of a localized affine operator, defined by similar meta and trainable parameters as the convolution, but which applies, for instance, in the 1D case, an affine mapping $\psi(\cdot\,;w) : \mathbb{R}^{D\times 1} \to \mathbb{R}^{D'\times K}$, to every $D \times 1$ sub-tensor of the input, and sums the shifted $D' \times K$ resulting tensors to compute its output. Such an operator increases the size of the signal and can be understood intuitively as a synthesis process (see Figure 4.1, right, and Figure 4.2, right).

A series of convolutional layers is the usual architecture to map a large-dimension signal, such as an image or a sound sample, to a low-dimension tensor. That can be, for instance, to get class scores for classification or a compressed representation. Transposed convolution layers are used the opposite way to build a large-dimension signal from a compressed representation, either to assess that the compressed representation contains enough information to build back the signal or for synthesis, as it is easier to learn a density model over a low-dimension representation. We will come back to this in § 5.2.

4.3 Activation functions

If a network were combining only linear components, it would itself be a linear operator, so it is essential to have non-linear operations. They are implemented in particular with activation functions, which are layers that transforms each component of the input tensor individually through a mapping, resulting in a tensor of the same shape.

There are many different activation functions, but the most used is the Rectified Linear Unit (ReLU) [Glorot et al., 2011], which sets negative values to zero and keeps positive values unchanged (see Figure 4.5, top right):

$$\mathrm{relu}(x) = \begin{cases} 0 & \text{if } x < 0, \\ x & \text{otherwise.} \end{cases}$$

Given that the core training strategy of deep-learning relies on the gradient, it may seem problematic to have a mapping that is not differentiable at zero and constant on half the real line. However, the main property gradient descent requires is that the gradient is informative on average. Parameter initialization and data normalization make half of the activations positive

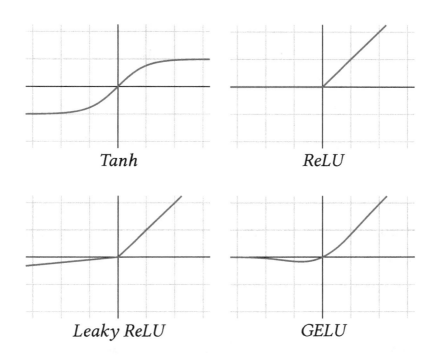

Figure 4.5: *Activation functions.*

when the training starts, ensuring that this is the case.

Before the generalization of ReLU, the standard activation function was the hyperbolic tangent (Tanh, see Figure 4.5, top left) which saturates exponentially fast on both the negative and the positive sides, aggravating the vanishing gradient.

Other popular activation functions follow the same idea of keeping positive values unchanged and squashing the negative values. Leaky ReLU

[Maas et al., 2013] applies a small positive multiplying factor to the negative values (see Figure 4.5, bottom left):

$$\text{leaky relu}(x) = \begin{cases} ax \text{ if } x < 0, \\ x \text{ otherwise.} \end{cases}$$

And GELU [Hendrycks and Gimpel, 2016] is defined with the cumulative distribution function of the Gaussian distribution, that is:

$$\text{gelu}(x) = xP(Z \leq x),$$

where $Z \sim \mathcal{N}(0,1)$. It roughly behaves like a smooth ReLU (see Figure 4.5, bottom right).

The choice of an activation function, in particular among the variants of ReLU, is generally driven by empirical performance.

4.4 Pooling

A classical strategy to reduce the signal size is to use a pooling operation that combines multiple activations into one that ideally summarizes the information. The most standard operation of this class is the max pooling layer, which, similarly to convolution, can operate in 1D and 2D, and is defined by a kernel size.

This layer computes the maximum activation per channel, over non-overlapping sub-tensors of spatial size equal to the kernel size. These values are stored in a result tensor with the same number of channels as the input, and whose spatial size is divided by the kernel size. As with the convolution, this operator has three meta-parameters: padding, stride, and dilation, with the stride being equal to the kernel size by default.

The max operation can be intuitively interpreted as a logical disjunction, or, when it follows a series of convolutional layer that compute local scores for the presence of parts, as a way of encoding that at least one instance of a part is present. It loses precise location, making it invariant to local deformations.

A standard alternative is the average pooling

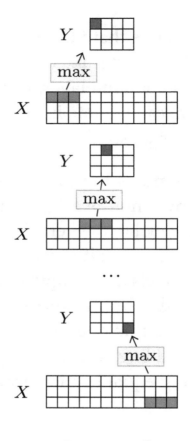

1D max pooling

Figure 4.6: *A 1D max pooling takes as input a $D \times T$ tensor X, computes the max over non-overlapping $1 \times L$ sub-tensors and stores the values in a resulting $D \times (T/L)$ tensor Y.*

layer that computes the average instead of the maximum over the sub-tensors. This is a linear operation, whereas max pooling is not.

4.5 Dropout

Some layers have been designed to explicitly facilitate training or improve the learned representations.

One of the main contributions of that sort was dropout [Srivastava et al., 2014]. Such a layer has no trainable parameters, but one meta-parameter, p, and takes as input a tensor of arbitrary shape.

It is usually switched off during testing, in which case its output is equal to its input. When it is active, it has a probability p to set to zero each activation of the input tensor independently, and it re-scales all the activations by a factor of $\frac{1}{1-p}$ to maintain the expected value unchanged (see Figure 4.7).

The motivation behind dropout is to favor meaningful individual activation and discourage group representation. Since the probability that a group of k activations remains intact through a dropout layer is $(1-p)^k$, joint representations become unreliable, which makes the training procedure avoid them. It can also be seen as a noise injection that makes the training more robust.

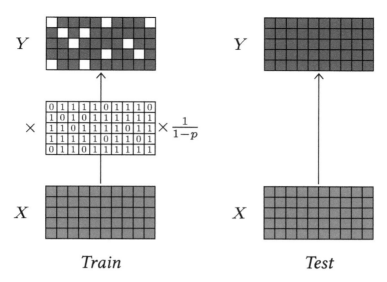

Figure 4.7: *Dropout can process a tensor of arbitrary shape. During training (left), it sets activations at random to zero with probability p and applies a multiplying factor to keep the expected values unchanged. During test (right), it keeps all the activations unchanged.*

When dealing with images and 2D tensors, the short-term correlation of the signals and the resulting redundancy negate the effect of dropout, since activations set to zero can be inferred from their neighbors. Hence, dropout for 2D tensors sets entire channels to zero instead of individual activations.

Although dropout is generally used to improve training and is inactive during inference, it can be used in certain setups as a randomization strategy, for instance, to estimate empirically confidence scores [Gal and Ghahramani, 2015].

4.6 Normalizing layers

An important class of operators to facilitate the training of deep architectures are the normalizing layers, which force the empirical mean and variance of groups of activations.

The main layer in that family is batch normalization [Ioffe and Szegedy, 2015] which is the only standard layer to process batches instead of individual samples. It is parameterized by a meta-parameter D and two series of trainable scalar parameters $\beta_1, \ldots, \beta_D$ and $\gamma_1, \ldots, \gamma_D$.

Given a batch of B samples $x_1, \ldots, x_B$ of dimension D, it first computes for each of the D components an empirical mean $\hat{m}_d$ and variance $\hat{v}_d$ across the batch:

$$\hat{m}_d = \frac{1}{B} \sum_{b=1}^{B} x_{b,d}$$

$$\hat{v}_d = \frac{1}{B} \sum_{b=1}^{B} (x_{b,d} - \hat{m}_d)^2,$$

from which it computes for every component $x_{b,d}$ a normalized value $z_{b,d}$, with empirical mean 0 and variance 1, and from it the final result value $y_{b,d}$ with mean β_d and standard de-

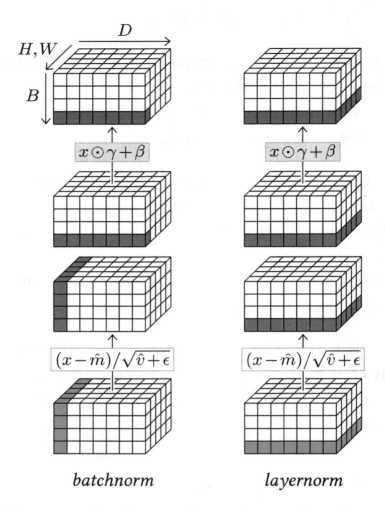

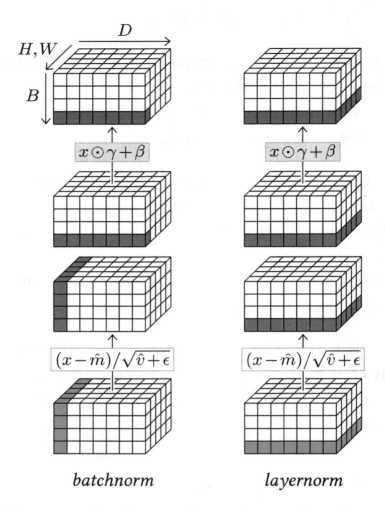

batchnorm   layernorm

Figure 4.8: *Batch normalization normalizes across the sample index dimension B and all spatial dimensions if any, so B, H, W for a $B \times D \times H \times W$ batch tensor, and scales/shifts according to D, which is implemented as a component-wise product by γ and a sum with β of the corresponding sub-tensors (left). Layer normalization normalizes across D and spatial dimensions, and scales/shifts according to the same (right).*

viation γ_d:

$$z_{b,d} = \frac{x_{b,d} - \hat{m}_d}{\sqrt{\hat{v}_d + \epsilon}}$$

$$y_{b,d} = \gamma_d z_{b,d} + \beta_d.$$

Because this normalization is defined across a batch, it is done only during training. During testing, the layer transforms individual samples according to the $\hat{m}_d$s and $\hat{v}_d$s estimated with a moving average over the full training set, which boils down to a fix affine transformation per component.

The motivation behind batch normalization was to avoid that a change in scaling in an early layer of the network during training impacts all the layers that follow, which then have to adapt their trainable parameters accordingly. Although the actual mode of action may be more complicated than this initial motivation, this layer considerably facilitates the training of deep models.

In the case of 2D tensors, to follow the principle of convolutional layers of processing all locations similarly, the normalization is done per-channel across all 2D positions, and β and γ remain vectors of dimension D so that the scaling/shift does not depend on the 2D position. Hence, if the tensor to process is of shape

$B \times D \times H \times W$, the layer computes $(\hat{m}_d, \hat{v}_d)$, for $d = 1, \ldots, D$ from the corresponding $B \times H \times W$ slice, normalizes it accordingly, and finally scales and shifts its components with the trainable parameters β_d and γ_d.

So, given a $B \times D$ tensor, batch normalization normalizes it across B and scales/shifts it according to D, which can be implemented as a component-wise product by γ and a sum with β. Given a $B \times D \times H \times W$ it normalizes across B, H, W and scales/shifts according to D (see Figure 4.8, left).

This can be generalized depending on these dimensions. For instance, layer normalization [Ba et al., 2016], computes moments and normalizes across all components of individual samples, and scales and shifts components individually (see Figure 4.8, right). So, given a $B \times D$ tensor, it normalizes across D and scales/shifts also according to D. Given a $B \times D \times H \times W$ tensor, it normalizes it across D, H, W and scales/shifts according to the same.

Contrary to batch normalization, since it processes samples individually, it behaves the same during training and testing.

4.7 Skip connections

Another technique that mitigates the vanishing gradient and allows the training of deep architectures are skip connections [Long et al., 2014; Ronneberger et al., 2015]. They are not layers per se, but an architectural design in which outputs of some layers are transported as-is to other layers further in the model, bypassing processing in-between. This unmodified signal can be concatenated or added to the input to the layer the connection branches into (see Figure 4.9). A particular type of skip connections is the residual connection which combines the signal with a sum, and usually skips only a few layers (see Figure 4.9, right).

The most desirable property of this design is to ensure that, even in the case of gradient-killing processing at a certain stage, the gradient will still propagate through the skip connections. Residual connections, in particular, allow for the building of deep models with up to several hundred layers, and key models, such as the residual networks [He et al., 2015] in computer vision (see § 5.2), and the Transformers [Vaswani et al., 2017] in natural language processing (see § 5.3), are entirely composed of blocks of layers with residual connections.

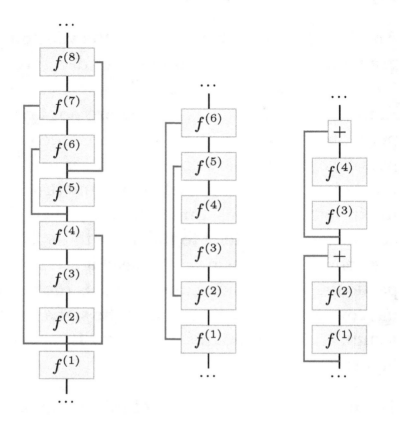

Figure 4.9: *Skip connections, highlighted in red on this figure, transport the signal unchanged across multiple layers. Some architectures (center) that downscale and re-upscale the representation size to operate at multiple scales, have skip connections to feed outputs from the early parts of the network to later layers operating at the same scales [Long et al., 2014; Ronneberger et al., 2015]. The residual connections (right) are a special type of skip connections that sum the original signal to the transformed one, and are usually short-term, bypassing at max a handful of layers [He et al., 2015].*

Their role can also be to facilitate multi-scale reasoning in models that reduce the signal size before re-expanding it, by connecting layers with compatible sizes. In the case of residual connections, they may also facilitate learning by simplifying the task to finding a differential improvement instead of a full update.

4.8 Attention layers

In many applications, there is a need for an operation able to combine local information at locations far apart in a tensor. For instance, this could be distant details for coherent and realistic image synthesis, or words at different positions in a paragraph to make a grammatical or semantic decision in natural language processing.

Fully connected layers cannot process large-dimension signals, nor signals of variable size, and convolutional layers are not able to propagate information quickly. Strategies that aggregate the results of convolutions, for instance, by averaging them over large spatial areas, suffer from mixing multiple signals into a limited number of dimensions.

Attention layers specifically address this problem by computing an attention score for each component of the resulting tensor to each component of the input tensor, without locality constraints, and averaging features across the full tensor accordingly [Vaswani et al., 2017].

Even though they are substantially more complicated than other layers, they have become a standard element in many recent models. They are, in particular, the key building block of Trans-

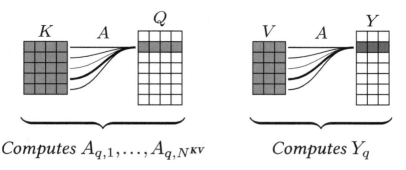

Computes $A_{q,1}, \ldots, A_{q,N^{KV}}$ Computes Y_q

Figure 4.10: *The attention operator can be interpreted as matching every query Q_q with all the keys $K_1, \ldots, K_{N^{KV}}$ to get normalized attention scores $A_{q,1}, \ldots, A_{q,N^{KV}}$ (left, and Equation 4.1), and then averaging the values $V_1, \ldots, V_{N^{KV}}$ with these scores to compute the resulting Y_q (right, and Equation 4.2).*

formers, the dominant architecture for Large Language Models. See § 5.3 and § 7.1.

Attention operator

Given

- a tensor Q of queries of size $N^Q \times D^{QK}$,
- a tensor K of keys of size $N^{KV} \times D^{QK}$, and
- a tensor V of values of size $N^{KV} \times D^V$,

the attention operator computes a tensor

$$Y = \mathrm{att}(K, Q, V)$$

of dimension $N^Q \times D^V$. To do so, it first computes for every query index q and every key index k an attention score $A_{q,k}$ as the <u>softargmax</u> of the dot products between the query Q_q and the keys:

$$A_{q,k} = \frac{\exp\left(\frac{1}{\sqrt{D^{QK}}}Q_q^\top K_k\right)}{\sum_l \exp\left(\frac{1}{\sqrt{D^{QK}}}Q_q^\top K_l\right)}, \qquad (4.1)$$

where the scaling factor $\frac{1}{\sqrt{D^{QK}}}$ keeps the range of values roughly unchanged even for large D^{QK}.

Then a retrieved value is computed for each query by averaging the values according to the attention scores (see Figure 4.10):

$$Y_q = \sum_k A_{q,k} V_k. \qquad (4.2)$$

So if a query Q_n matches one key K_m far more than all the others, the corresponding attention score $A_{n,m}$ will be close to one, and the retrieved value Y_n will be the value V_m associated to that key. But, if it matches several keys equally, then Y_n will be the average of the associated values.

This can be implemented as

$$\mathrm{att}(Q,K,V) = \underbrace{\mathrm{softargmax}\left(\frac{QK^\top}{\sqrt{D^{QK}}}\right)}_{A} V.$$

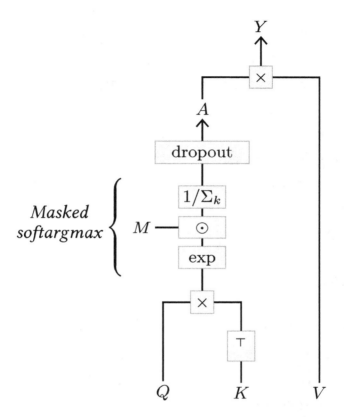

Figure 4.11: *The attention operator* $Y = \mathrm{att}(Q, K, V)$ *computes first an attention matrix* A *as the per-query softargmax of* $QK^{\top}$, *which may be masked by a constant matrix* M *before the normalization. This attention matrix goes through a dropout layer before being multiplied by* V *to get the resulting* Y. *This operator can be made* <u>causal</u> *by taking* M *full of* 1s *below the diagonal and zero above.*

This operator is usually extended in two ways, as depicted in Figure 4.11. First, the attention matrix can be masked by multiplying it before the softargmax normalization by a Boolean matrix M. This allows, for instance, to make the operator <u>causal</u> by taking M full of 1s below the diagonal and zero above, preventing Y_q from depending on keys and values of indices k greater than q. Second, the attention matrix is processed by a <u>dropout layer</u> (see § 4.5) before being multiplied by V, providing the usual benefits during training.

Multi-head Attention Layer

This parameterless attention operator is the key element in the <u>Multi-Head Attention layer</u> depicted in Figure 4.12. This layer has for meta-parameters a number H of heads, and the shapes of three series of H trainable weight matrices

- W^Q of size $H \times D \times D^{QK}$,
- W^K of size $H \times D \times D^{QK}$, and
- W^V of size $H \times D \times D^V$,

to compute respectively the queries, the keys, and the values from the input, and a final weight matrix W^O of size $HD^V \times D$ to aggregate the per-head results.

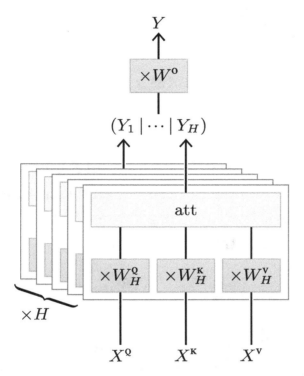

Figure 4.12: *The Multi-head Attention layer applies for each of its $h = 1, \ldots, H$ heads a parametrized linear transformation to individual elements of the input sequences X^Q, X^K, X^V to get sequences Q, K, V that are processed by the attention operator to compute Y_h. These H sequences are concatenated along features, and individual elements are passed through one last linear operator to get the final result sequence Y.*

It takes as input three sequences

- X^{Q} of size $N^{\mathrm{Q}} \times D$,
- X^{K} of size $N^{\mathrm{KV}} \times D$, and
- X^{V} of size $N^{\mathrm{KV}} \times D$,

from which it computes, for $h = 1, \ldots, H$,

$$Y_h = \mathrm{att}\left(X^{\mathrm{Q}} W_h^{\mathrm{Q}}, X^{\mathrm{K}} W_h^{\mathrm{K}}, X^{\mathrm{V}} W_h^{\mathrm{V}}\right).$$

These sequences $Y_1, \ldots, Y_H$ are concatenated along the feature dimension and each individual element of the resulting sequence is multiplied by W^{O} to get the final result:

$$Y = (Y_1 \mid \cdots \mid Y_H) W^{\mathrm{O}}.$$

As we will see in § 5.3 and in Figure 5.6, this layer is used to build two model sub-structures: self-attention blocks, in which the three input sequences X^{Q}, X^{K}, and X^{V} are the same, and cross-attention blocks, where X^{K} and X^{V} are the same.

It is noteworthy that the attention operator, and consequently the multi-head attention layer when there is no masking, is invariant to a permutation of the keys and values, and equivariant to a permutation of the queries, as it would permute the resulting tensor similarly.

4.9 Token embedding

In many situations, we need to convert discrete tokens into vectors. This can be done with an embedding layer, which consists of a lookup table that directly maps integers to vectors.

Such a layer is defined by two meta-parameters: the number N of possible token values, and the dimension D of the output vectors, and one trainable $N \times D$ weight matrix M.

Given as input an integer tensor X of dimension $D_1 \times \cdots \times D_K$ and values in $\{0, \ldots, N-1\}$ such a layer returns a real-valued tensor Y of dimension $D_1 \times \cdots \times D_K \times D$ with

$$\forall d_1, \ldots, d_K,$$
$$Y[d_1, \ldots, d_K] = M[X[d_1, \ldots, d_K]].$$

4.10 Positional encoding

While the processing of a fully connected layer is specific to both the positions of the features in the input tensor and to the position of the resulting activation in the output tensor, convolutional layers and Multi-Head Attention layers are oblivious to the absolute position in the tensor. This is key to their strong invariance and inductive bias, which is beneficial for dealing with a stationary signal.

However, this can be an issue in certain situations where proper processing has to access the absolute positioning. This is the case, for instance, for image synthesis, where the statistics of a scene are not totally stationary, or in natural language processing, where the relative positions of words strongly modulate the meaning of a sentence.

The standard way of coping with this problem is to add or concatenate a positional encoding, which is a feature vector that depends on the location, to the feature representation at every position. This positional encoding can be learned as other layer parameters, or defined analytically.

For instance, in the original Transformer model, for a series of vectors of dimension D, Vaswani et al. [2017] add an encoding of the sequence index as a series of sines and cosines at various frequencies:

$$\text{pos-enc}[t, d] = \begin{cases} \sin\left(\frac{t}{T^{d/D}}\right) & \text{if } d \in 2\mathbb{N} \\ \cos\left(\frac{t}{T^{(d-1)/D}}\right) & \text{otherwise,} \end{cases}$$

with $T = 10^4$.

Chapter 5
Architectures

The field of deep learning has developed over the years for each application domain multiple deep architectures that exhibit good trade-offs with respect to multiple criteria of interest: e.g. ease of training, accuracy of prediction, memory footprint, computational cost, scalability.

5.1 Multi-Layer Perceptrons

The simplest deep architecture is the Multi-Layer Perceptron (MLP), which takes the form of a succession of fully connected layers separated by activation functions. See an example in Figure 5.1. For historical reasons, in such a model, the number of hidden layers refers to the number of linear layers, excluding the last one.

A key theoretical result is the universal approximation theorem [Cybenko, 1989] which states that, if the activation function σ is continuous

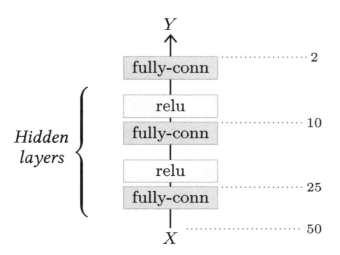

Figure 5.1: *This multi-layer perceptron takes as input a one dimension tensor of size* 50, *is composed of three fully connected layers with outputs of dimensions respectively* 25, 10, *and* 2, *the two first followed by ReLU layers.*

and not polynomial, any continuous function f can be approximated arbitrarily well uniformly on a compact domain, that is bounded and containing its boundary, by a model of the form $l_2 \circ \sigma \circ l_1$ where l_1 and l_2 are affine. Such a model is a MLP with a single hidden layer, and this result implies that it can approximate anything of practical value. However, this approximation holds if the dimension of the first linear layer's output can be arbitrarily large.

In spite of their simplicity, MLPs remain an important tool when the dimension of the signal to be processed is not too large.

5.2 Convolutional networks

The standard architecture for processing images is a convolutional network, or convnet, that combines multiple convolutional layers, either to reduce the signal size before it can be processed by fully connected layers, or to output a 2D signal also of large size.

LeNet-like

The original LeNet model for image classification [LeCun et al., 1998] combines a series of 2D convolutional layers and max pooling layers that play the role of feature extractor, with a series of fully connected layers which act like a MLP and perform the classification per se (see Figure 5.2).

This architecture was the blueprint for many models that share its structure and are simply larger, such as AlexNet [Krizhevsky et al., 2012] or the VGG family [Simonyan and Zisserman, 2014].

Residual networks

Standard convolutional neural networks that follow the architecture of the LeNet family are not easily extended to deep architectures and suffer

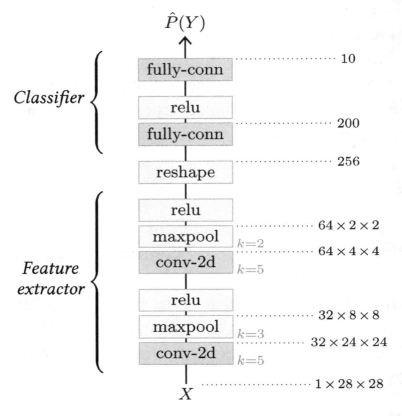

Figure 5.2: *Example of a small LeNet-like network for classifying 28×28 grayscale images of handwritten digits [LeCun et al., 1998]. Its first half is convolutional, and alternates convolutional layers per se and max pooling layers, reducing the signal dimension for 28×28 scalars to 256. Its second half processes this 256 dimension feature vector through a one hidden layer perceptron to compute 10 logit scores corresponding to the ten possible digits.*

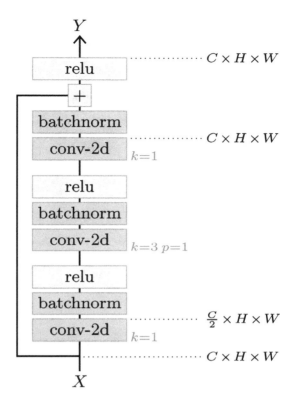

Figure 5.3: *A residual block.*

from the vanishing gradient problem. The residual networks, or ResNets, proposed by He et al. [2015] explicitly address the issue of the vanishing gradient with residual connections (see § 4.7), that allow hundreds of layers. They have become standard architectures for computer vision applications, and exist in multiple versions depending on the number of layers. We are going to look in detail at the architecture of the ResNet-50 for classification.

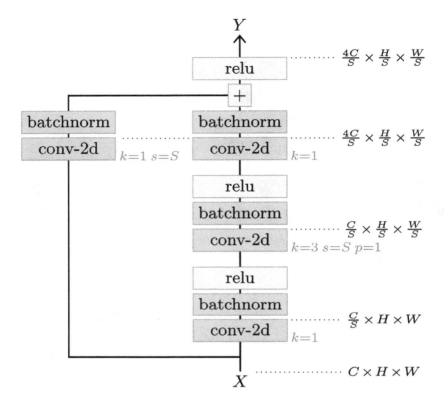

Figure 5.4: *A downscaling residual block. It admits a meta-parameter S, the stride of the first convolution layer, which modulates the reduction of the tensor size.*

As other ResNets, it is composed of a series of residual blocks, each combining several convolutional layers, batch norm layers, and ReLU layers, wrapped in a residual connection. Such a block is pictured in Figure 5.3.

A key requirement for high performance with real images is to propagate a signal with a large number of channels, to allow for a rich repre-

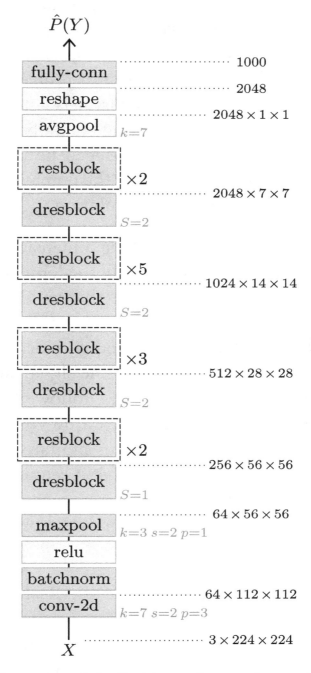

Figure 5.5: *Structure of the ResNet-50 [He et al., 2015].*

sentation. However, the parameter count of a convolutional layer, and its computational cost, are quadratic with the number of channels. This residual block mitigates this problem by first reducing the number of channels with a 1×1 convolution, then operating spatially with a 3×3 convolution on this reduced number of channels, and then upscaling the number of channels, again with a 1×1 convolution.

The network reduces the dimensionality of the signal to finally compute the logits for the classification. This is done thanks to an architecture composed of several sections, each starting with a downscaling residual block that halves the height and width of the signal, and doubles the number of channels, followed by a series of residual blocks. Such a downscaling residual block has a structure similar to a standard residual block, except that it requires a residual connection that changes the tensor shape. This is achieved with a 1×1 convolution with a stride of two (see Figure 5.4).

The overall structure of the ResNet-50 is presented in Figure 5.5. It starts with a 7×7 convolutional layer that converts the three-channel input image to a 64-channel image of half the size, followed by four sections of residual blocks. Surprisingly, in the first section, there is no down-scaling, only an increase of the number of channels by a factor of 4. The output of the last residual block is $2048 \times 7 \times 7$, which is converted to a vector of dimension 2048 by an average pooling of kernel size 7×7, and then processed through a fully connected layer to get the final logits, here for 1000 classes.

5.3   Attention models

As stated in § 4.8, many applications, in particular from natural language processing, greatly benefit from models that include attention mechanisms. The architecture of choice for such tasks, which has been instrumental in recent advances in deep learning, is the Transformer proposed by Vaswani et al. [2017].

Transformer

The original Transformer, pictured in Figure 5.7, was designed for sequence-to-sequence translation. It combines an encoder that processes the input sequence to get a refined representation, and an autoregressive decoder that generates each token of the result sequence, given the encoder's representation of the input sequence and the output tokens generated so far. As the residual convolutional networks of § 5.2, both the encoder and the decoder of the Transformer are sequences of compounded blocks built with residual connections.

The self-attention block, pictured on the left of Figure 5.6, combines a Multi-Head Attention layer (see § 4.8), that recombines information globally, allowing any position to collect infor-

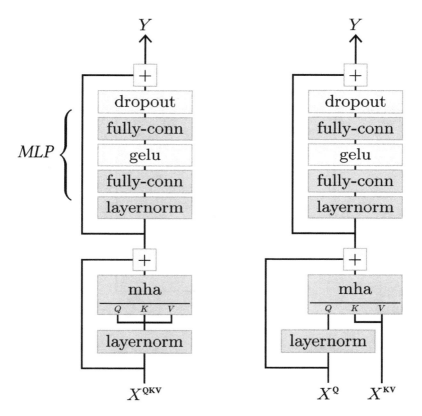

Figure 5.6: *Self-attention block (left) and cross-atten-tion block (right). These specific structures proposed by* Radford et al. [2018] *differ slightly from the original architecture of* Vaswani et al. [2017]*, in particular by having the layer normalization first in the residual blocks.*

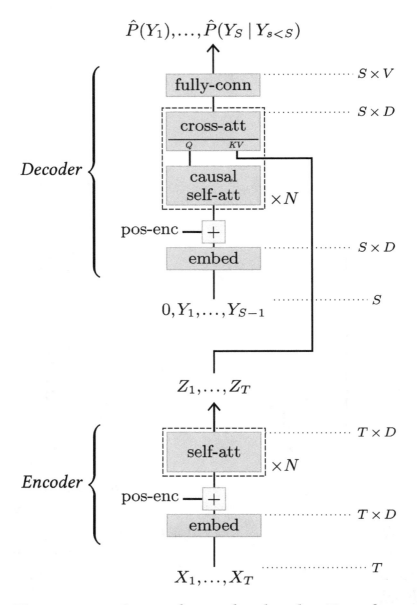

Figure 5.7: *Original encoder-decoder __Transformer__ model for sequence-to-sequence translation [Vaswani et al., 2017].*

mation from any other positions, with a one-hidden-layer MLP that updates representations at every position separately. This block can be made causal by using an adequate attention mask, as described in § 4.8

The cross-attention block, pictured on the right of Figure 5.6, is similar except that it takes as input two sequences, one to compute the queries and one to compute the keys and values.

The encoder of the Transformer (see Figure 5.7, bottom), recodes the input sequence of discrete tokens $X_1, \ldots X_T$ with an embedding layer (see § 4.9), and adds a positional encoding (see § 4.10), before processing it with several self-attention blocks to generate a refined representation $Z_1, \ldots, Z_T$.

The decoder (see Figure 5.7, top), takes as input the sequence $Y_1, \ldots, Y_{S-1}$ of result tokens produced so far, similarly recodes them through an embedding layer, adds a positional encoding, and processes it through alternating causal self-attention blocks and cross-attention blocks to produce the logits predicting the next tokens. These cross-attention blocks compute their keys and values from the encoder's result representation $Z_1, \ldots, Z_T$, which allows the resulting se-

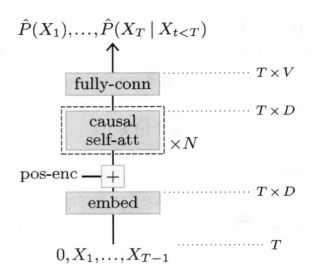

Figure 5.8: *GPT model [Radford et al., 2018].*

quence to be a function of the original sequence $X_1,\ldots,X_T$.

As we saw in § 3.2 being <u>causal</u> ensures that such a model can be trained by minimizing the cross-entropy summed across the full sequence.

Generative Pre-trained Transformer

The <u>Generative Pre-trained Transformer</u> (GPT) [Radford et al., 2018, 2019], pictured in Figure 5.8 is a pure autoregressive model that consists of a succession of causal self-attention blocks, hence a causal version of the original Transformer encoder. We come back to how they are used for text generation in § 7.1.

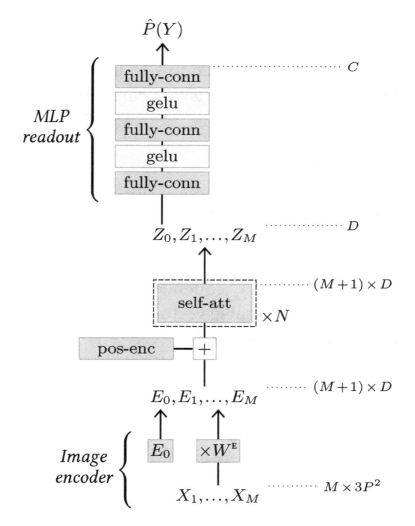

Figure 5.9: *Vision Transformer model [Dosovitskiy et al., 2020].*

This class of models scales extremely well, up to hundreds of billions of trainable parameters [Brown et al., 2020].

Vision Transformer

Transformers have been put to use for image classification with the Vision Transformer (ViT) model [Dosovitskiy et al., 2020] (see Figure 5.9).

It splits the three-channel input image into M patches of resolution $P \times P$, which are then flattened to create a sequence of vectors $X_1, \ldots, X_M$ of shape $M \times 3P^2$. This sequence is multiplied by a trainable matrix W^E of shape $3P^2 \times D$ to map it to a $M \times D$ sequence, to which is concatenated one trainable vector E_0. The resulting $(M+1) \times D$ sequence $E_0, \ldots, E_M$ is then processed through multiple self-attention blocks. See § 5.3 and Figure 5.6.

The first element Z_0 in the resultant sequence, which corresponds to E_0 and is not associated which any part of the image, is finally processed by a two-hidden-layer MLP to get the final C logits. Such a token, added for a readout of a class prediction, was introduced by Devlin et al. [2018] in the BERT model and is referred to as a CLS token.

PART III

APPLICATIONS

Chapter 6
Prediction

A first category of applications, such as face recognition, sentiment analysis, object detection, or speech recognition, requires predicting an unknown value from an available signal.

6.1 Image denoising

A direct application of deep models to image processing is to recover from degradation by utilizing the redundancy in the statistical structure of images. The petals of a sunflower on a grayscale picture can be colored with high confidence, and the texture of a geometric shape such as a table on a low-light grainy picture can be corrected by averaging it over a large area likely to be uniform.

A denoising autoencoder is a model that takes as input a degraded signal $\tilde{X}$ and computes an estimate of the original one X. For images, it is a convolutional network that may integrate skip-connections, in particular to combine representations at the same resolution obtained early and late in the model, and attention layers to facilitate taking into account elements far away from each other.

Such a model is trained by collecting a large number of clean samples paired with their degraded inputs. The latter can be captured in degraded conditions, such as low-light or inadequate focus, or generated algorithmically, for instance, by converting the clean sample to grayscale, reducing its size, or compressing it aggressively with a lossy compression method.

The standard training procedure for denoising autoencoders uses the MSE loss summed across all pixels, in which case the model aims at computing the best average clean picture, given the degraded one, that is $\mathbb{E}[X \mid \tilde{X}]$. This quantity may be problematic when X is not completely determined by $\tilde{X}$, in which case some parts of the generated signal may be an unrealistic, blurry average.

6.2 Image classification

Image classification is the simplest strategy for extracting semantics from an image and consists of predicting a class from a finite, predefined number of classes, given an input image.

The standard models for this task are convolutional networks, such as ResNets (see § 5.2), and attention-based models such as ViT (see § 5.3). Those models generate a vector of logits with as many dimensions as there are classes.

The training procedure simply minimizes the cross-entropy loss (see § 3.1). Usually, performance can be improved with data augmentation, which consists of modifying the training samples with hand-designed random transformations that do not change the semantic content of the image, such as cropping, scaling, mirroring, or color changes.

6.3 Object detection

A more complex task for image understanding is object detection, in which the objective is, given an input image, to predict the classes and positions of objects of interest.

An object position is formalized as the four coordinates (x_1, y_1, x_2, y_2) of a rectangular bounding box, and the ground truth associated with each training image is a list of such bounding boxes, each labeled with the class of the object in it.

The standard approach to solve this task, for instance, by the Single Shot Detector (SSD) [Liu et al., 2015]), is to use a convolutional neural network that produces a sequence of image representations Z_s of size $D_s \times H_s \times W_s$, $s = 1, \dots, S$, with decreasing spatial resolution $H_s \times W_s$ down to 1×1 for $s = S$ (see Figure 6.1). Each of those tensors covers the input image in full, so the h, w indices correspond to a partitioning of the image lattice into regular squares that gets coarser when s increases. As seen in § 4.2, and illustrated in Figure 4.4, due to the succession of convolutional layers, a feature vector $(Z_s[0, h, w], \dots, Z_s[D_s - 1, h, w])$ is a descriptor of an area of the image, called its receptive field, that is larger than this square but centered on

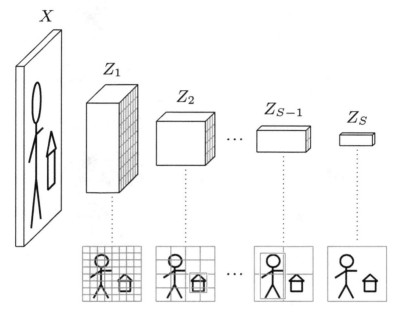

Figure 6.1: *A convolutional object detector processes the input image to generate a sequence of representations of decreasing resolutions. It computes for every h, w, at every scale s, a pre-defined number of bounding boxes whose centers are in the image area corresponding to that cell, and whose size are such that they fit in its receptive field. Each prediction takes the form of the estimates $(\hat{x}_1, \hat{x}_2, \hat{y}_1, \hat{y}_2)$, represented by the red boxes above, and a vector of $C+1$ logits for the C classes of interest, and an additional "no object" class.*

Figure 6.2: *Examples of object detection with the Single-Shot Detector [Liu et al., 2015].*

it. This results in a non-ambiguous matching of any bounding box (x_1, x_2, y_1, y_2) to a s, h, w, determined respectively by $\max(x_2 - x_1, y_2 - y_1)$, $\frac{y_1 + y_2}{2}$, and $\frac{x_1 + x_2}{2}$.

Detection is achieved by adding S convolutional layers, each processing a Z_s and computing for every tensor indices h, w the coordinates of a bounding box, and the associated logits. If there are C object classes, there are $C + 1$ logits, the additional one standing for "no object." Hence, each additional convolution layer has $4 + C + 1$ output channels. The SSD algorithm in particular generates several bounding boxes per s, h, w, each dedicated to a hard-coded range of aspect ratios.

Training sets for object detection are costly to create, since the labeling with bounding boxes requires a slow human intervention. To mitigate this issue, the standard approach is to start with a convolutional model that has been pre-trained on a large classification data set such as VGG-16 for the original SSD, and to replace its final fully connected layers with additional convolutional ones. Surprisingly, models trained for classification only have learned feature representations that can be repurposed for object detection, even though that task involves the regression of geometric quantities.

During training, every ground-truth bounding box is associated with its s, h, w, and induces a loss term composed of a cross-entropy loss for the logits, and a regression loss such as MSE for the bounding box coordinates. Every other s, h, w free of bounding-box match induces a cross-entropy only penalty to predict the class "no object".

6.4   Semantic segmentation

The finest-grain prediction task for image understanding is semantic segmentation, which consists of predicting, for every pixel, the class of the
object to which it belongs. This can be achieved
with a standard convolutional neural network
that outputs a convolutional map with as many
channels as classes, carrying the estimated logits
for every pixel.

While a standard residual network, for instance,
can generate a dense output of the same resolution as its input, as for object detection, this
task requires operating at multiple scales. This
is necessary so that any object, or sufficiently
informative sub-part, regardless of its size, is
captured somewhere in the model by the feature
representation at a single tensor position. Hence,
standard architectures for that task downscale
the image with a series of convolutional layers
to increase the receptive field of the activations,
and re-upscale it with a series of transposed convolutional layers, or other upscaling methods
such as bilinear interpolation, to make the prediction at high resolution.

However, a strict downscaling-upscaling architecture does not allow for operating at a fine

Figure 6.3: *Semantic segmentation results with the Pyramid Scene Parsing Network [Zhao et al., 2016].*

grain when making the final prediction, since all the signal has been transmitted through a low-resolution representation at some point. Models that apply such downscaling-upscaling serially mitigate these issues with skip connections from layers at a certain resolution, before downscaling, to layers at the same resolution, after upscaling [Long et al., 2014; Ronneberger et al., 2015]. Models that do it in parallel, after a convolutional backbone, concatenate the resulting multi-scale representation after upscaling, before making the final per-pixel prediction [Zhao et al., 2016].

Training is achieved with a standard cross-entropy summed over all the pixels. As for object detection, training can start from a network pre-trained on a large-scale image classification data set to compensate for the limited availability of segmentation ground truth.

6.5 Speech recognition

Speech recognition consists of converting a sound sample into a sequence of words. There have been plenty of approaches to this problem historically, but a conceptually simple and recent one proposed by Radford et al. [2022] consists of casting it as a sequence-to-sequence translation and then solving it with a standard attention-based Transformer, as described in § 5.3.

Their model first converts the sound signal into a spectrogram, which is a one-dimensional series $T \times D$, that encodes at every time step a vector of energies in D frequency bands. The associated text is encoded with the BPE tokenizer (see § 3.2).

The spectrogram is processed through a few 1D convolutional layers, and the resulting representation is fed into the encoder of the Transformer. The decoder directly generates a discrete sequence of tokens, that correspond to one of the possible tasks considered during training. Multiple objectives are considered for training: transcription of English or non-English text, translation from any language to English, or detection of non-speech sequences, such as background music or ambient noise.

This approach allows leveraging extremely large data sets that combine multiple types of sound sources with diverse ground truth.

It is noteworthy that even though the ultimate goal of this approach is to produce a translation as deterministic as possible given the input signal, it is formally the sampling of a text distribution conditioned on a sound sample, hence a synthesis process. The decoder is in fact extremely similar to the generative model of § 7.1.

6.6 Text-image representations

A powerful approach to image understanding consists of learning consistent image and text representations, such that an image, or a textual description of it, would be mapped to the same feature vector.

The Contrastive Language-Image Pre-training (CLIP) proposed by Radford et al. [2021] combines an image encoder f, which is a ViT, and a text encoder g, which is a GPT. See § 5.3 for both.

To repurpose a GPT as a text encoder, instead of a standard autoregressive model, they add to the input sequence an "end of sentence" token, and use the representation of this token in the last layer as the embedding. Both embeddings have the same dimension, which, depending on the configuration, is between 512 and 1024.

Those two models are trained from scratch using a data set of 400 million image-text pairs (i_k, t_k) collected from the internet. The training procedure follows the standard mini-batch stochastic gradient descent approach but relies on a contrastive loss. The embeddings are computed for every image and every text of the N pairs in the mini-batch, and a cosine similarity measure is computed not only between text and image embeddings from each pair, but also across pairs, resulting in an $N \times N$ matrix of similarity scores:

$$l_{m,n} = f(i_m)^\top g(t_n), \, m = 1,\ldots,N, n = 1,\ldots,N.$$

The model is trained with cross-entropy so that, $\forall n$ the values $l_{1,n},\ldots,l_{N,n}$ interpreted as logit scores predict n, and similarly for $l_{n,1},\ldots,l_{n,N}$. This means that $\forall n,m$, s.t. $n \neq m$ the similarity $l_{n,n}$ is unambiguously greater than both $l_{n,m}$ and $l_{m,n}$.

When it has been trained, this model can be used to do zero-shot prediction, that is, classifying a signal in the absence of training examples by defining a series of candidate classes with text descriptions, and computing the similarity of the embedding of an image with the embedding of each of those descriptions (see Figure 6.4).

Additionally, since the textual descriptions are often detailed, such a model has to capture a richer representation of images and pick up cues overlooked by classifier networks. This translates to excellent performance on challenging datasets such as ImageNet Adversarial [Hendrycks et al., 2019] which was specifically designed to degrade or erase cues on which standard predictors rely.

Figure 6.4: *The CLIP text-image embedding [Radford et al., 2021] allows to do zero-shot prediction by predicting what class description embedding is the most consistent with the image embedding.*

Chapter 7
Synthesis

A second category of applications distinct from prediction is synthesis. It consists of fitting a density model to training samples and providing means to sample from this model.

7.1 Text generation

The standard approach to text synthesis is to use an attention-based, autoregressive model. The most successful in this domain is the GPT [Radford et al., 2018], which we described in § 5.3.

The encoding into tokens and the decoding is done with the BPE tokenizer (see § 3.2).

When it has been trained on very large datasets, a Large Language Model (LLM) exhibits extremely powerful properties. Besides the syntactic and grammatical structure of the language, it has to integrate very diverse knowledge, e.g. to predict the word following "The capital of Japan is", "if water is heated to 100 Celsius degrees it turns into", or "because her puppy was sick, Jane was".

This results in particular in the ability to solve zero-shot prediction, where no training example is available and the objective is defined in natural language, e.g. "In the following sentences, indicate which ones are aggressive." More surprisingly, when such a model is put in a statistical context by a "prompt" carefully crafted, it can exhibit abilities for question answering, problem solving, and chain-of-thought that appear eerily close to high-level reasoning [Chowdhery et al.,

2022; Bubeck et al., 2023].

Due to these remarkable capabilities, these models are sometimes referred to as foundation models [Bommasani et al., 2021].

7.2   *Image generation*

Multiple deep methods have been developed to model and sample from a high-dimensional density. A powerful approach for image synthesis relies on inverting a diffusion process.

The principle consists of defining analytically a process that gradually degrades any sample, and consequently transforms the complex and unknown density of the data into a simple and well-known density such as a normal, and training a deep architecture to invert this degradation process [Ho et al., 2020].

Given a fixed T, the diffusion process defines a probabilities over series of $T+1$ images as follows: samples x_0 uniformly in the data set, and then go on sampling $x_{t+1} \sim p(x_{t+1} \mid x_t)$ where the conditional distribution p is defined analytically, and such that it gradually erases the structure that was in x_0. The setup should be such that the distribution $p(x_T)$ of x_T has a simple, known form, so in particular does not depend on the complicated data distribution $p(x_0)$, and can be sampled.

For instance, Ho et al. [2020] normalize the data to have a mean of 0 and a variance of 1, and their diffusion process consists of adding a bit of white

x_T

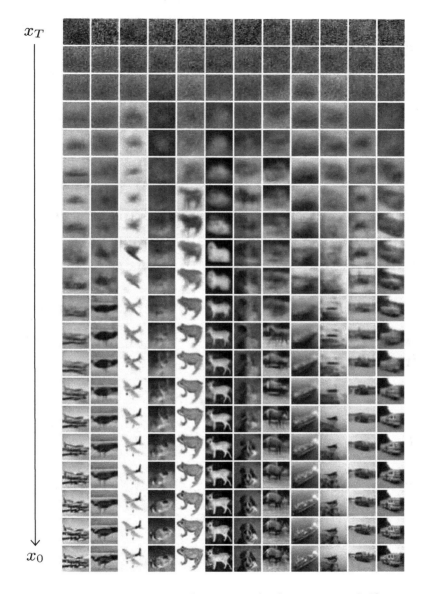

x_0

Figure 7.1: *Image synthesis with denoising diffusion* [*Ho et al., 2020*]. *Each sample starts as a white noise* x_T *(top), and is gradually de-noised by sampling iteratively* $x_{t-1} \mid x_t \sim \mathcal{N}(x_t + f(x_t, t; w), \sigma_t)$.

noise and re-normalizing the variance to 1. This process exponentially reduces the importance of x_0, and x_t's density can rapidly be approximated with a normal.

The denoiser f is a deep architecture that should model and allow sampling from, $f(x_{t-1}, x_t, t; w) \simeq p(x_{t-1} \mid x_t)$. It can be shown, thanks to a variational bound, that if this one-step reverse process is accurate enough, sampling $x_T \sim p(x_T)$ and denoising T steps with f results in a x_0 that follows $p(x_0)$.

Training f can be achieved by generating a large number of sequences $x_0^{(n)}, \ldots, x_T^{(n)}$, picking a t_n in each, and maximizing

$$\sum_n \log f(x_{t_n-1}^{(n)}, x_{t_n}^{(n)}, t_n; w).$$

Given their diffusion process, Ho et al. [2020] have a denoising of the form:

$$x_{t-1} \mid x_t \sim \mathcal{N}(x_t + f(x_t, t; w); \sigma_t), \qquad (7.1)$$

where σ_t is defined analytically.

In practice, such a model initially hallucinates structures by pure luck in the random noise, and then gradually build more elements that emerge from the noise by reinforcing the most likely continuation of the image obtained thus far.

This approach can be extended to text-conditioned synthesis, to generate images that match a description. For instance, Nichol et al. [2021] add to the mean of the denoising distribution of Equation 7.1 a bias that goes in the direction of increasing the CLIP matching score (see § 6.6) between the produced image and the conditioning text description.

The missing bits

For the sake of concision, this volume skips many important topics, in particular:

Recurrent Neural Networks

Before attention models showed greater performance, Recurrent Neural Networks (RNN) were the standard approach for dealing with temporal sequences such as text or sound samples. These architectures possess an internal hidden state that gets updated every time a component of the sequence is processed. Their main components are layers such as LSTM [Hochreiter and Schmidhuber, 1997] or GRU [Cho et al., 2014].

Training a recurrent architecture amounts to unfolding it in time, which results in a long composition of operators. This has historically prompted the design of key techniques now used for deep architectures such as rectifiers and gating, a form of skip connections which are modulated dynamically.

Autoencoder

An autoencoder is a model that maps an input signal, possibly of high dimension, to a low-dimension latent representation, and then maps it back to the original signal, ensuring that information has been preserved. We saw it in § 6.1 for denoising, but it can also be used to automatically discover a meaningful low-dimension parameterization of the data manifold.

The Variational Autoencoder (VAE) proposed by Kingma and Welling [2013] is a generative model with a similar structure. It imposes, through the loss, a pre-defined distribution to the latent representation. This allows, after training, the generation of new samples by sampling the latent representation according to this imposed distribution and then mapping back through the decoder.

Generative Adversarial Networks

Another approach to density modeling is the Generative Adversarial Networks (GAN) introduced by Goodfellow et al. [2014]. This method combines a generator, which takes a random input following a fixed distribution as input and produces a structured signal such as an image, and a discriminator, which takes as input a sample and predicts whether it comes from the training set or if it was generated by the generator.

Training optimizes the discriminator to minimize a standard cross-entropy loss, and the generator to maximize the discriminator's loss. It can be shown that at equilibrium the generator produces samples indistinguishable from real data. In practice, when the gradient flows through the discriminator to the generator, it informs the latter about the cues that the discriminator uses that should be addressed.

Reinforcement Learning

Many problems require a model to estimate an accumulated long-term reward given action choices and an observable state, and what actions to choose to maximize that reward. Reinforcement Learning (RL) is the standard framework to formalize such problems, and strategy games or robotic control, for instance, can be formulated within it. Deep models, particularly convolutional neural networks, have demonstrated excellent performance for this class of tasks [Mnih et al., 2015].

Fine-tuning

As we saw in § 6.3 for object detection, and in § 6.4 for semantic segmentation, starting form a pre-trained model and fine-tuning it to the task at hand is an efficient strategy to deal with small training sets.

Furthermore, due to the dramatic increase in the size of architectures, particularly that of Large Language Models (see Figure 3.7), training a single model can cost several millions of dollars, and fine-tuning is a crucial, and often the only way, to achieve high performance on a specific task.

Graph Neural Networks

Many applications require processing signals which are not organized regularly on a grid. For instance, molecules, proteins, 3D meshes, or geographic locations are more naturally structured as graphs. Standard convolutional networks or even attention models are poorly adapted to process such data, and the tool of choice for such a task is Graph Neural Networks (GNN) [Scarselli et al., 2009].

These models are composed of layers that compute activations at each vertex by combining linearly the activations located at its immediate neighboring vertices. This operation is very similar to a standard convolution, except that the data structure does not reflect any geometrical information associated with the feature vectors they carry.

Self-supervised training

As stated in § 7.1, even though they are trained only to predict the next word, Large Language Models trained on large unlabeled data sets such as GPT (see § 5.3) are able to solve various tasks such as identifying the grammatical role of a word, answering questions, or even translating from one language to another [Radford et al., 2019].

Such models constitute one category of a larger class of methods that fall under the name of self-supervised learning, and try to take advantage of unlabeled data sets [Balestriero et al., 2023].

The key principle of these methods is to define a task that does not require labels but necessitates feature representations which are useful for the real task of interest, for which a small labeled data set exists. In computer vision, for instance, a standard approach consists of optimizing image features so that they are invariant to data transformations that do not change the semantic content of the image, while being statistically uncorrelated [Zbontar et al., 2021].

Afterword

Recent developments in Artificial Intelligence have been incredibly exciting, and it is difficult to comment on them without being overly dramatic. There are few doubts that these technologies will cause fundamental changes in how we work, how we interact with knowledge and information, and that they will force us to rethink concepts as fundamental as intelligence, understanding, and sentience.

In spite of its weaknesses, particularly its sheer brutality and its computational cost, deep learning is likely to remain an important component of AI systems for the foreseeable future and, as such, a key element of this new era.

Bibliography

J. L. Ba, J. R. Kiros, and G. E. Hinton. Layer Normalization. *CoRR*, abs/1607.06450, 2016. [pdf]. 81

R. Balestriero, M. Ibrahim, V. Sobal, et al. A Cookbook of Self-Supervised Learning. *CoRR*, abs/2304.12210, 2023. [pdf]. 141

A. Baydin, B. Pearlmutter, A. Radul, and J. Siskind. Automatic differentiation in machine learning: a survey. *CoRR*, abs/1502.05767, 2015. [pdf]. 41

M. Belkin, D. Hsu, S. Ma, and S. Mandal. Reconciling modern machine learning and the bias-variance trade-off. *CoRR*, abs/1812.11118, 2018. [pdf]. 49

R. Bommasani, D. Hudson, E. Adeli, et al. On the Opportunities and Risks of Foundation Models. *CoRR*, abs/2108.07258, 2021. [pdf]. 132

T. Brown, B. Mann, N. Ryder, et al. Language Models are Few-Shot Learners. *CoRR*, abs/2005.14165, 2020. [pdf]. 52, 110

S. Bubeck, V. Chandrasekaran, R. Eldan, et al. Sparks of Artificial General Intelligence: Early experiments with GPT-4. *CoRR*, abs/2303.12712, 2023. [pdf]. 132

T. Chen, B. Xu, C. Zhang, and C. Guestrin. Training Deep Nets with Sublinear Memory Cost. *CoRR*, abs/1604.06174, 2016. [pdf]. 42

K. Cho, B. van Merrienboer, Ç. Gülçehre, et al. Learning Phrase Representations using RNN Encoder-Decoder for Statistical Machine Translation. *CoRR*, abs/1406.1078, 2014. [pdf]. 137

A. Chowdhery, S. Narang, J. Devlin, et al. PaLM: Scaling Language Modeling with Pathways. *CoRR*, abs/2204.02311, 2022. [pdf]. 52, 131

G. Cybenko. Approximation by superpositions of a sigmoidal function. *Mathematics of Control, Signals, and Systems*, 2(4):303–314, December 1989. [pdf]. 96

J. Devlin, M. Chang, K. Lee, and K. Toutanova. BERT: Pre-training of Deep Bidirectional

Transformers for Language Understanding. *CoRR*, abs/1810.04805, 2018. [pdf]. 52, 111

A. Dosovitskiy, L. Beyer, A. Kolesnikov, et al. An Image is Worth 16x16 Words: Transformers for Image Recognition at Scale. *CoRR*, abs/2010.11929, 2020. [pdf]. 110, 111

K. Fukushima. Neocognitron: A self-organizing neural network model for a mechanism of pattern recognition unaffected by shift in position. *Biological Cybernetics*, 36(4):193–202, April 1980. [pdf]. 2

Y. Gal and Z. Ghahramani. Dropout as a Bayesian Approximation: Representing Model Uncertainty in Deep Learning. *CoRR*, abs/1506.02142, 2015. [pdf]. 77

X. Glorot and Y. Bengio. Understanding the difficulty of training deep feedforward neural networks. In *International Conference on Artificial Intelligence and Statistics (AISTATS)*, 2010. [pdf]. 43, 60

X. Glorot, A. Bordes, and Y. Bengio. Deep Sparse Rectifier Neural Networks. In *International Conference on Artificial Intelligence and Statistics (AISTATS)*, 2011. [pdf]. 69

A. Gomez, M. Ren, R. Urtasun, and R. Grosse. The Reversible Residual Network: Backpropagation Without Storing Activations. *CoRR*, abs/1707.04585, 2017. [pdf]. 42

I. J. Goodfellow, J. Pouget-Abadie, M. Mirza, et al. Generative Adversarial Networks. *CoRR*, abs/1406.2661, 2014. [pdf]. 138

K. He, X. Zhang, S. Ren, and J. Sun. Deep Residual Learning for Image Recognition. *CoRR*, abs/1512.03385, 2015. [pdf]. 50, 82, 83, 100, 102

D. Hendrycks and K. Gimpel. Gaussian Error Linear Units (GELUs). *CoRR*, abs/1606.08415, 2016. [pdf]. 71

D. Hendrycks, K. Zhao, S. Basart, et al. Natural Adversarial Examples. *CoRR*, abs/1907.07174, 2019. [pdf]. 128

J. Ho, A. Jain, and P. Abbeel. Denoising Diffusion Probabilistic Models. *CoRR*, abs/2006.11239, 2020. [pdf]. 133, 134, 135

S. Hochreiter and J. Schmidhuber. Long Short-Term Memory. *Neural Computation*, 9(8):1735–1780, 1997. [pdf]. 137

S. Ioffe and C. Szegedy. Batch Normalization: Accelerating Deep Network Training by Reducing Internal Covariate Shift. In *International Conference on Machine Learning (ICML)*, 2015. [pdf]. 78

J. Kaplan, S. McCandlish, T. Henighan, et al. Scaling Laws for Neural Language Models. *CoRR*, abs/2001.08361, 2020. [pdf]. 50, 51

D. Kingma and J. Ba. Adam: A Method for Stochastic Optimization. *CoRR*, abs/1412.6980, 2014. [pdf]. 38

D. P. Kingma and M. Welling. Auto-Encoding Variational Bayes. *CoRR*, abs/1312.6114, 2013. [pdf]. 138

A. Krizhevsky, I. Sutskever, and G. Hinton. ImageNet Classification with Deep Convolutional Neural Networks. In *Neural Information Processing Systems (NIPS)*, 2012. [pdf]. 8, 98

Y. LeCun, B. Boser, J. S. Denker, et al. Backpropagation applied to handwritten zip code recognition. *Neural Computation*, 1(4):541–551, 1989. [pdf]. 8

Y. LeCun, L. Bottou, Y. Bengio, and P. Haffner. Gradient-based learning applied to document recognition. *Proceedings of the IEEE*, 86(11): 2278–2324, 1998. [pdf]. 98, 99

W. Liu, D. Anguelov, D. Erhan, et al. SSD: Single Shot MultiBox Detector. *CoRR*, abs/1512.02325, 2015. [pdf]. 117, 119

J. Long, E. Shelhamer, and T. Darrell. Fully Convolutional Networks for Semantic Segmentation. *CoRR*, abs/1411.4038, 2014. [pdf]. 82, 83, 123

A. L. Maas, A. Y. Hannun, and A. Y. Ng. Rectifier nonlinearities improve neural network acoustic models. In *proceedings of the ICML Workshop on Deep Learning for Audio, Speech and Language Processing*, 2013. [pdf]. 71

V. Mnih, K. Kavukcuoglu, D. Silver, et al. Human-level control through deep reinforcement learning. *Nature*, 518(7540):529–533, February 2015. [pdf]. 139

A. Nichol, P. Dhariwal, A. Ramesh, et al. GLIDE: Towards Photorealistic Image Generation and Editing with Text-Guided Diffusion Models. *CoRR*, abs/2112.10741, 2021. [pdf]. 136

A. Radford, J. Kim, C. Hallacy, et al. Learning Transferable Visual Models From Natural

Language Supervision. *CoRR*, abs/2103.00020, 2021. [pdf]. 127, 129

A. Radford, J. Kim, T. Xu, et al. Robust Speech Recognition via Large-Scale Weak Supervision. *CoRR*, abs/2212.04356, 2022. [pdf]. 125

A. Radford, K. Narasimhan, T. Salimans, and I. Sutskever. Improving Language Understanding by Generative Pre-Training, 2018. [pdf]. 106, 109, 131

A. Radford, J. Wu, R. Child, et al. Language Models are Unsupervised Multitask Learners, 2019. [pdf]. 109, 141

O. Ronneberger, P. Fischer, and T. Brox. U-Net: Convolutional Networks for Biomedical Image Segmentation. In *Medical Image Computing and Computer-Assisted Intervention*, 2015. [pdf]. 82, 83, 123

F. Scarselli, M. Gori, A. C. Tsoi, et al. The Graph Neural Network Model. *IEEE Transactions on Neural Networks (TNN)*, 20(1):61–80, 2009. [pdf]. 140

R. Sennrich, B. Haddow, and A. Birch. Neural Machine Translation of Rare Words with Subword Units. *CoRR*, abs/1508.07909, 2015. [pdf]. 33

J. Sevilla, L. Heim, A. Ho, et al. Compute Trends Across Three Eras of Machine Learning. *CoRR*, abs/2202.05924, 2022. [pdf]. 9, 50, 52

J. Sevilla, P. Villalobos, J. F. Cerón, et al. Parameter, Compute and Data Trends in Machine Learning, May 2023. [web]. 53

K. Simonyan and A. Zisserman. Very Deep Convolutional Networks for Large-Scale Image Recognition. *CoRR*, abs/1409.1556, 2014. [pdf]. 98

N. Srivastava, G. Hinton, A. Krizhevsky, et al. Dropout: A Simple Way to Prevent Neural Networks from Overfitting. *Journal of Machine Learning Research (JMLR)*, 15:1929–1958, 2014. [pdf]. 75

M. Telgarsky. Benefits of depth in neural networks. *CoRR*, abs/1602.04485, 2016. [pdf]. 46

A. Vaswani, N. Shazeer, N. Parmar, et al. Attention Is All You Need. *CoRR*, abs/1706.03762, 2017. [pdf]. 82, 85, 93, 105, 106, 107

J. Zbontar, L. Jing, I. Misra, et al. Barlow Twins: Self-Supervised Learning via Redundancy Reduction. *CoRR*, abs/2103.03230, 2021. [pdf]. 142

M. D. Zeiler and R. Fergus. Visualizing and Understanding Convolutional Networks. In *European Conference on Computer Vision (ECCV)*, 2014. [pdf]. 67

H. Zhao, J. Shi, X. Qi, et al. Pyramid Scene Parsing Network. *CoRR*, abs/1612.01105, 2016. [pdf]. 123, 124

Index

1D convolution, 64
2D convolution, 64

activation, 23, 40
    function, 69, 96
    map, 66
Adam, 38
affine operation, 59
artificial neural network, 8, 11
attention operator, 86
autoencoder, 138
    denoising, 114
Autograd, 41
autoregressive model, *see* model, autoregressive
average pooling, 72

backpropagation, 41
backward pass, 41
basis function regression, 14
batch, 21, 37
batch normalization, 78, 101
bias vector, 59, 64

BPE, *see* Byte Pair Encoding
Byte Pair Encoding, 33, 125, 131

cache memory, 21
capacity, 16
causal, 32, 88, 108
    model, *see* model, causal
chain rule (derivative), 39
chain rule (probability), 30
channel, 23
checkpointing, 42
classification, 18, 26, 98, 116
CLIP, *see* Contrastive Language-Image
        Pre-training
CLS token, 111
computational cost, 42
Contrastive Language-Image Pre-training, 127
contrastive loss, 27, 127
convnet, *see* convolutional network
convolution, 64
convolutional layer, *see* layer, convolutional
convolutional network, 98
cross-attention block, 91, 106, 108
cross-entropy, 27, 32, 44

data augmentation, 116
deep learning, 8, 11
denoising autoencoder, *see* autoencoder,
        denoising

density modeling, 18
depth, 40
diffusion process, 133
dilation, 65, 72
discriminator, 139
downscaling residual block, 103
dropout, 75, 89

embedding layer, *see* layer, embedding
epoch, 47

filter, 64
fine-tuning, 140
flops, 22
forward pass, 40
foundation model, 132
FP32, 22
framework, 23

GAN, *see* Generative Adversarial Networks
GELU, 71
Generative Adversarial Networks, 138
Generative Pre-trained Transformer, 109, 127,
        131, 141
generator, 138
GNN, *see* Graph Neural Network
GPT, *see* Generative Pre-trained Transformer
GPU, *see* Graphical Processing Unit
gradient descent, 34, 36, 39, 44
gradient step, 34

Graph Neural Network, 140
Graphical Processing Unit, 8, 20
ground truth, 18

hidden layer, *see* layer, hidden
hidden state, 137
hyperbolic tangent, 70

image processing, 98
image synthesis, 85, 133
inductive bias, 17, 48, 64

kernel size, 64, 72
key, 86

Large Language Model, 54, 86, 131, 140, 141
layer, 40, 57
    attention, 85
    convolutional, 64, 72, 85, 93, 98, 101, 117,
        122, 125
    embedding, 92, 108
    fully connected, 59, 85, 93, 96, 98
    hidden, 96
    linear, 59
    Multi-Head Attention, 89, 93, 105
    normalizing, 78
    reversible, 42
layer normalization, 81
Leaky ReLU, 70
learning rate, 34

learning rate schedule, 49
LeNet, 98, 99
linear layer, *see* layer, linear
LLM, *see* Large Language Model
local minimum, 34
logit, 26
loss, 12

machine learning, 11, 17, 18
max pooling, 72
mean squared error, 14, 26
memory requirement, 42
memory speed, 21
meta parameter, *see* parameter, meta
metric learning, 27
MLP, *see* multi-layer perceptron
model, 12
    autoregressive, 30, 31, 131
    causal, 31, 89, 108, 109
    parametric, 12
    pre-trained, 120, 124, 140
multi-layer perceptron, 44, 96, 108

natural language processing, 85
NLP, *see* natural language processing
non-linearity, 69
normalizing layer, *see* layer, normalizing

object detection, 117
overfitting, 17, 47

padding, 65, 72

parameter, 12

    meta, 13, 47

parametric model, *see* model, parametric

peak performance, 22

pooling, 72

positional encoding, 93, 108

posterior probability, 26

pre-trained model, *see* model, pre-trained

query, 86

random initialization, 60

receptive field, 66, 117

rectified linear unit, 69, 137

recurrent neural network, 137

regression, 18

Reinforcement Learning, 139

reinforcement learning, 139

ReLU, *see* rectified linear unit

residual

    block, 101

    connection, 82, 100

    network, 46, 82, 100

ResNet-50, 100

reversible layer, *see* layer, reversible

RL, *see* Reinforcement Learning

RNN, *see* recurrent neural network

scaling laws, 50

self-attention block, 91, 105, 106

self-supervised learning, 141

semantic segmentation, 122

SGD, *see* stochastic gradient descent

Single Shot Detector, 117

skip connection, 82, 123, 137

softargmax, 26, 87

softmax, 26

speech recognition, 125

SSD, *see* Single Shot Detector

stochastic gradient descent, 37, 44, 50

stride, 65, 72

supervised learning, 19

Tanh, *see* hyperbolic tangent

tensor, 23

tensor cores, 21

Tensor Processing Unit, 21

test set, 47

text synthesis, 131

token, 30

tokenizer, 33, 125, 131

TPU, *see* Tensor Processing Unit

trainable parameter, 12, 23, 50

training, 12

training set, 12, 25, 47

Transformer, 46, 82, 86, 93, 105, 107, 125

transposed convolution, 67, 122

underfitting, 16
universal approximation theorem, 96
unsupervised learning, 19

VAE, *see* variational, autoencoder
validation set, 47
value, 86
vanishing gradient, 43, 56
variational
    autoencoder, 138
    bound, 135
Vision Transformer, 111, 127
ViT, *see* Vision Transformer
vocabulary, 30

weight, 13
weight decay, 28
weight matrix, 59

zero-shot prediction, 128, 131

Preprint–June 18, 2023

Printed in the USA
CPSIA information can be obtained
at www.ICGtesting.com
LVHW051233020823
753722LV00005B/65